JAMES
MARTIN

james's
DESSERTS

PHOTOGRAPHY BY
PETER CASSIDY

 ALHAMBRA
EDITIONS

PUBLISHING DIRECTOR Jane O'Shea
CREATIVE DIRECTOR Helen Lewis
EDITOR AND PROJECT MANAGER
Gillian Haslam, Jamie Ambrose
EDITORIAL ASSISTANT Romilly Morgan
DESIGNERS Katherine Keeble, Ros Holder
PHOTOGRAPHER Peter Cassidy
PRODUCTION DIRECTOR Vincent Smith
PRODUCTION CONTROLLER
Leonie Kellman

First published as *Desserts* in 2007
by Quadrille Publishing Limited
This edition first published in 2013 by
Alhambra Editions
Alhambra House
27-31 Charing Cross Road
London WC2H 0LS

Text © James Martin 2007, 2013
Photography © Peter Cassidy 2007
Design and layout ©
    Quadrille Publishing Ltd 2013

Cataloguing in Publication Data: a catalogue
record for this book is available from the
British Library.

ISBN 978 184949 298 0

Printed in China

This is the book I've been wanting to write for over a decade. It's a compilation of all my favourite desserts, including recipes that have been in my family for generations, classic dishes, traditional favourites that I've given a new twist to, plus lots of recipes that I've developed from scratch. The desserts range from warming comfort food such as sticky toffee pudding (how can anyone resist that?) and white chocolate, whisky and croissant pudding, to light, summery dishes such as apple or mango sorbet and raspberry puff pastry stack. There are homely puds, including individual apple and blueberry pies and spicy plum crumble, and the classics found on many restaurants menus – lemon tart, chocolate profiteroles, even Black Forest gâteau which deserves a new lease of life. There are cakes and bakes you can put together in a matter of minutes, plus celebration cakes such as the white chocolate wedding cake.

This book has developed from a television series, *Sweet Baby James*, which I filmed in various places around the UK. While on my travels for the show, I visited Lucy's of Amblesides deli and restaurant in the Lake District. There she holds a monthly pudding night called 'Up the Duff Pudding Night', when only puddings are served to all the diners. I say 'puddings' as in 'more than one' – I was actually served six, one after another. They all arrived at the table hot and loaded with cream. First was a clotted cream rice pudding, rich and creamy with the skin on the top (just how it should be) to prove it had been cooked in the oven and not subjected to the microwave. Next up was a rhubarb crumble, again with cream, followed by a banana fruit-cake pud, also hot and served with cream. At this point my belt gave way to my belly and I had to call it a night, but the 12 women I was with battled on with another three puds.

These pudding-only nights are nothing new in the US; New York eateries serving only desserts are opening all the time, and the trend is spreading to Europe. It just goes to prove real puddings hold a special place in our hearts and many fond memories. They can either remind you of school dinners or Mum's or Gran's special dessert surprise. The Hot Puddings chapter is full of these classics and modern twists on dishes that have been around for years. There are dishes like peach Melba that's been given the modern chef treatment but still retains all the elements that combine to make it such a great dish. I've also simplified troublesome dishes such as the soufflé – everyone's nightmare dinner-party dish, but when it's made with bought-in custard I promise you can't fail. In the Tarts and Flans chapter, you'll find apple pie – the nation's favourite pudding – served with blueberries, the new super fruit according to the healthy-eating experts, plus many other ideas for both new and old pastry-based dishes.

Not so many years back, most households used to have a baking day but now it's sad to see so many people resorting to buying the plastic-coated, dried rubbish from the supermarket. The art of baking isn't a science; it's one of knowledge and practice, and if you were to ask chefs what they remember of their childhood food, homemade cakes and biscuits would come up in the conversation. I know they would in mine. That's why I love visiting the WI stalls at fairs and shows around the UK: they bring back so many great memories of my gran and auntie, who were both amazing pastry cooks. None of my family were chefs, just great cooks, and that's why we can learn something by just visiting these cake stalls selling great food cooked with love by a generation who really understand the art of good baking. Take a look at the Cakes and Bakes chapter where you'll find plenty of recipes to tempt you into baking again.

The Cold Puddings chapter is for all those people who come up to me to say the reason for not making desserts is the lack of time. The chapter is full of stuff you can make in advance and even leave in the freezer for a week or two. There are desserts you can take your time over in order to get them right as well as simpler ones to make in minutes. It's the same with many of the recipes in the Ice Creams and Sorbets chapter – most of them can be made in advance.

If you want to learn the real art of true cooking, you start at the beginning. Many people think pastry is a science, but it's all about understanding the basics and knowing why things do what they do. For me, it's where my passion for cooking first began. As a young kid, I'd watch my gran rubbing butter and flour together in a bowl balanced on her knees while she watched a whole episode of *Coronation Street*, always listening to the show but never distracted from the task in hand. Her pastry was better then any pastry I've ever tasted since, and that's down to the way the fat was incorporated into the flour. You wouldn't think that a small thing like that would make such a difference, but it does. Follow my recipes in the Basics chapter, and you, too, can master the not-so-difficult task of pastry-making.

So flick through the pages in this book – you're guaranteed to find plenty to tempt you back into the kitchen.

basics

rich shortcrust
PASTRY

MAKES 300G

Mix together the flour and salt (and icing sugar if making sweet pastry). Add half the cubed butter to the flour. Gently and swiftly rub the fat into the flour until it resembles coarse breadcrumbs. Add the rest of the butter and mix until it's the size of small peas. Make a well in the centre of the dry ingredients.

Mix the egg with the lemon juice and water and pour into the well a little at a time, rubbing it through your fingers, until it forms a dough (you may not need all the liquid). Turn onto a floured board and knead lightly until smooth. Shape into a ball, wrap in cling film and refrigerate for at least 30 minutes before rolling out.

To line a tin or mould, roll the chilled pastry onto the rolling pin, then unroll over the tin, draping the pastry into the tin or mould. Gently press it in place using your fingers.

200g plain flour
¼ tsp salt
2 tbsp icing sugar (if making
sweet pastry)
100g cold unsalted butter, cubed
1 egg, beaten
1 tsp lemon juice
2 tbsp ice water

To get shortcrust with that crumble-in-the-mouth texture, make it by hand rather then by machine. A mixer overworks the gluten in the flour, causing the pastry to shrink when cooked.

simple rough
PUFF PASTRY

MAKES 350G

Mix together the flour and salt. Cut the butter into small cubes and mix the butter into the flour without breaking up the lumps. Mix to a stiff dough with the water and lemon juice.

On a floured board, roll the dough into a rectangle three times as long as it is wide – about 30 x 10cm.

Fold the top third down and the bottom third up. Turn the pastry sideways and seal the edges. Continue to roll and fold four times, leaving the pastry to rest for 15 minutes between each folding and rolling. Wrap in cling film and leave to rest and chill in the fridge for 30 minutes before using.

200g plain flour
¼ tsp salt
150g butter
100ml cold water
1 tsp lemon juice

Until ready-made all-butter puff pastry is more widely available in the shops, this recipe is all you need for great-tasting puff pastry.

choux
PASTRY

Preheat the oven to 220°C/425°F/Gas mark 7. Put the water, milk, diced butter, salt and sugar in a saucepan set over a high heat and boil for 1 minute, stirring with a spatula. Turn off the heat and, stirring all the time, quickly add the flour until the mixture is very smooth.

When the mixture is smooth, place the pan over the heat and stir with the spatula for 1 minute. The paste will begin to poach and some of the water will evaporate. Don't let the paste dry out too much, or it will crack during cooking. Immediately add the eggs off the heat, one at a time, mixing in with a spatula.

Stir well with the spatula until the eggs are thoroughly combined and the paste has a very smooth texture. It is now ready to use.

Carefully spoon the mixture into a large piping bag fitted with a plain 1cm nozzle.

Pipe out the paste onto baking parchment or a greased baking tray. Smooth down any bumps on the piped pastry with a finger dipped in water. Pipe small buns if making profiteroles or longer shapes if you're making eclairs.

Place the baking tray in the oven, then throw half a cup of water onto the oven floor to create some steam. Bake in the oven, opening the oven door slightly (about 1–2cm) after 5 minutes for a few seconds. Cooking time will vary from 10–20 minutes, depending on the size of the buns or eclairs.

125ml water
125ml milk
100g butter, cut into small pieces
3g fine salt
5g caster sugar
150g flour, sifted
4 medium eggs

victoria
SPONGE

MAKES 2 x 20CM CAKES

Preheat the oven to 190°C/375°F/Gas mark 5. Grease and flour two 20cm sandwich tins. Place the butter, caster sugar and vanilla extract into a bowl or blender and mix well to a creamy consistency.

Then slowly mix the eggs into the bowl, adding them one by one.

Fold in the flour. When mixed, pour into the tins and bake for 20–25 minutes until well risen and golden brown. The cakes should spring back when pressed on top with a finger. Turn out and leave to cool on wire racks.

200g butter, plus extra
   for greasing
200g caster sugar
½ tsp vanilla extract
4 medium eggs
200g self-raising flour

Named after Queen Victoria, this cake can be made in two ways but using the same basic ingredients. One method mixes the eggs and sugar together first, as in a Génoese sponge; the other method, used here, creams the butter and sugar together like a bun mixture. The results are very different, but if you want a lighter cake, then use this method.

shortbread

Dice the butter and put it into a mixing bowl to soften. Sift the flour on top with the caster sugar, a pinch of salt and the vanilla seeds. Rub together gently and form into a ball. Alternatively, blitz all the ingredients in a food processor until they come together into a ball.

Lightly flour the work surface, then roll out the shortbread mixture until it is about 5mm thick. Prick all over the surface with a fork.

Using a sharp knife, cut the shortbread into fingers measuring about 5cm in length and about 1.5cm wide. Carefully lift onto a baking tray and rest in the fridge for 30 minutes or so.

Preheat the oven to 180°C/350°F/Gas mark 4. Dust the shortbread with a little caster sugar before baking. Bake for 20 minutes, or until golden brown and firm to the touch. Leave until completely cooled before removing from the baking tray.

225g chilled unsalted butter,
    plus extra for greasing
225g flour, plus extra for dusting
60g caster sugar, plus extra
    for dusting
pinch of salt
½ vanilla pod, seeds only

The secret to good shortbread is to mix the dough as little as possible and chill it after mixing. The best way to bake it is in a low oven, so that it doesn't colouring too much. For citrus-flavoured shortbread add the zest of 2 lemons or oranges in step 1.

spun
SUGAR

Put the sugar in a very clean, non-stick pan and place over a medium heat. Do not stir. When the sugar starts to turn into a caramel, tilt the pan to mix the sugar as it starts to turn so that it blends together. When all the sugar is at a caramel colour and has dissolved, remove the pan from the heat and place the base of the pan in cold water to cool. Don't allow any water in the pan. As the sugar cools, it will become thicker and resemble golden syrup. If it thickens too much, gently reheat.

100g white caster sugar

To make spirals, take a tablespoon of sugar and quickly twirl the sugar trail around a cook's steel. Snap off the tail of the sugar and carefully slide the spiral off the steel. Place on a baking tray to set.

To make spun sugar, take a tablespoon of the sugar and spin it very quickly backwards and forwards over a cook's steel or a rolling pin. Quickly lift the sugar up and scoop into a bundle. Place on a baking tray to set.

To make pulled sugar, take a tablespoon of the sugar and allow it to fall off the spoon. Pinch the sugar trail between your thumb and forefinger (it will be hot!). Working quickly, pinch two or three strands on top of each other. Snap off the sugar trail when you have made a small bundle. Place on a baking tray to set.

To make a basket, grease a small glass bowl or ladle with olive oil (don't use vegetable oil as it's too thin). Take a tablespoon of sugar and criss-cross the mould with the sugar trail. Leave the sugar to set on the mould, then carefully lift the basket off and fill with your chosen dessert, such as ice cream or sorbet.

hot MERINGUE

MAKES 1 PAVLOVA, 1 BAKED ALASKA OR 10 MERINGUE NESTS

Preheat the oven to 200°C/400°F/Gas mark 6. Pour the sugar onto a baking tray and place in the oven to warm up.

350g white caster sugar
6 egg whites

When the sugar has been in the oven for 5 minutes, beat the egg whites in an electric mixer until stiff. Take the sugar out of the oven.

When the egg whites are well-risen and firm, set the mixer to the lowest speed and gently pour on the hot sugar in a thin stream, taking no more than 2 minutes to add all the sugar. The meringue is now ready to use.

cold MERINGUE

MAKES 1 PAVLOVA, 1 BAKED ALASKA OR 10 MERINGUE NESTS

Preheat the oven to 140°C/275°F/Gas mark 1. Line a baking tray with baking parchment or a non-stick baking mat.

6 large egg whites
250g white caster sugar

Put the egg whites in a large clean bowl and, using an electric whisk on a low speed, begin whisking. Continue for about 2 minutes until the whites are foamy, then switch the speed to medium and carry on whisking until the egg whites reach the stiff-peak stage. Next, whisk the sugar in on high speed, a dessertspoon at a time, until you have a stiff and glossy mixture.

Spoon the mixture onto the baking tray, place in the centre of the oven and leave it for 1 hour. Turn the oven off and leave the meringues to dry out in the oven until completely cold.

italian
MERINGUE

Pour the water into a pan, then add the sugar and glucose, if using. Place over a moderate heat and stir the mixture until it boils. Skim the surface and wash down the sugar crystals which form inside the pan with a brush dipped in cold water. Now increase the heat so that the syrup cooks rapidly. Insert the sugar thermometer to check the temperature.

When the sugar reaches 110°C/225°F, beat the egg whites in an electric mixer until stiff. Take the sugar off the heat when it reaches 121°C/250°F.

When the egg whites are well-risen and firm, set the mixer to the lowest speed and gently pour on the cooked sugar in a thin stream, taking care not to let it run onto the whisks. Continue to beat at low speed until the mixture is almost completely cold – this will take about 15 minutes. The meringue is now ready to use.

80ml water
360g white caster sugar
30g glucose (optional)
6 egg whites

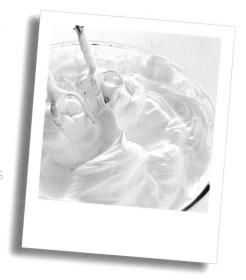

The smoothest meringue comes from the Italian method; the boiling sugar cooks the egg whites when it's added to them. It does take a lot of whisking, but I think it's worth the effort.

raspberry
SAUCE

MAKES 150ML

To me, this method makes a fresher-tasting sauce than cooking the berries in the sugar and water, which makes the sauce taste more like jam. Simply tip the raspberries and the sugar into a blender, add the water and purée well until smooth.

Place a sieve over a bowl and pour the blended purée through to strain out all the seeds.

Use a spatula to press the sauce through if necessary. Store the sauce in a covered container in the fridge and use as required.

250g fresh raspberries
2 tbsp icing sugar
50ml water

fresh
CUSTARD

MAKES 750ML

Beat the egg yolks and sugar together in a bowl until well blended.

Pour the milk and cream in a saucepan. Split and scrape the inside of the vanilla pod into the milk and cream and bring to the boil.

Once the milk and cream are boiling, pour a little onto the eggs and mix well, then pour back into the pan. Return to the heat and, using a whisk, lightly stir the mix to thicken; do not boil.

As the egg yolks warm, the cream will thicken to create a custard. Keep stirring until it coats the back of the spoon. Remove from the heat and pass through a sieve and leave to cool. The custard can now be served warm, or stirred occasionally until it cools.

8 egg yolks
75g caster sugar
300ml milk
300ml double cream
1 vanilla pod, split

The most important thing here is to make sure the mixture doesn't boil when the eggs are added. You need to heat it up just enough to cook the eggs.

hot
PUDDINGS

croissant
BUTTER PUDDING

SERVES 4

Preheat the oven to 180°C/350°F/Gas mark 4.

Pour the milk and cream into a pan, add the vanilla pod, and gradually bring to the boil.

Put the eggs, egg yolks and sugar in a food-mixer bowl and mix gently using the whisk attachment on a low setting.

While the cream is heating, slice the croissants and place in an ovenproof dish, slightly overlapping the pieces. Sprinkle with sultanas and pour over the butter.

Once the cream has boiled, take it off the heat. Add the egg mixture and chocolate and stir well. Place to one side off the heat to allow the chocolate to melt, stirring occasionally.

Add the whisky to the cream mixture. Using a sieve, strain the cream over the croissants and bake in the oven for 20–25 minutes, or until almost set.

Remove from the oven and dust with icing sugar. Caramelize the topping using a very hot grill or, if you have one, a blowtorch. This is best served at room temperature, with a spoonful of ice cream.

500ml milk
500ml double cream
1 vanilla pod
3 whole eggs
6 egg yolks
200g caster sugar
6 large croissants
25g sultanas
25g butter, melted
175g white chocolate,
    cut into shards
75ml whisky
icing sugar, for dusting

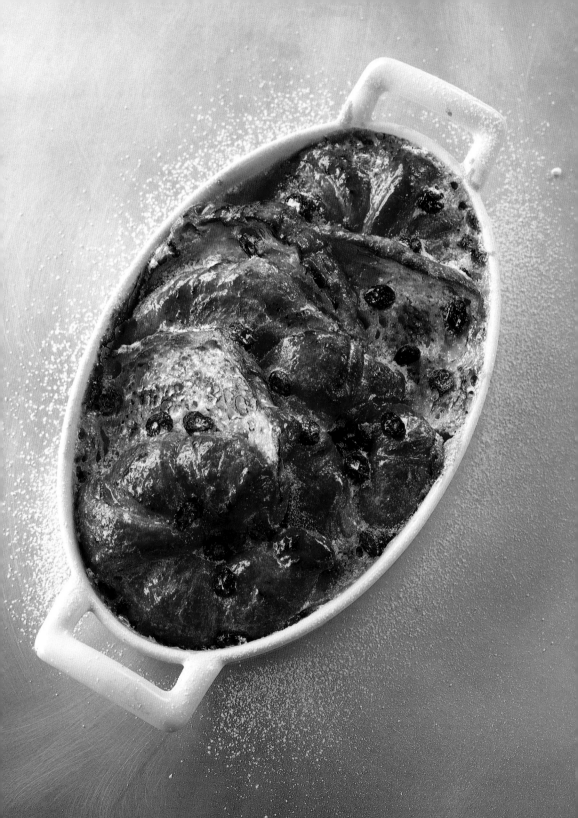

apple &
BLUEBERRY PIE

Preheat the oven to 200°C/400°F/Gas mark 6. Grease six 7.5cm dariole moulds.

Roll out two-thirds of the pastry on a floured work surface and cut out circles slightly larger than the moulds. Line the greased moulds with pastry.

Peel, quarter and core the apples, then slice them thickly into a bowl with three-quarters of the sugar and all the lemon juice and zest. Stir gently to mix.

Heat a pan and add the apples with the butter and remaining sugar. Cook for 3–4 minutes, then add the blueberries. Cook for a few more minutes, then remove from the heat and cool.

When cool, fill the pastry-lined moulds with the filling.

Roll out the remaining pastry approximately 1cm larger than the moulds and place it on top of the filling. Seal the edges well and then make a small hole in the top to allow the steam to escape.

Make decorations from any pastry trimmings (I like to make a few leaves) and seal them with a little water. Brush the tops of the pies with beaten egg, then dust with caster sugar. Bake for 15 minutes until the fruit is tender and the top is golden brown. Serve hot with clotted cream or ice cream.

450g rich shortcrust pastry
  (see page 12)
flour, for dusting
550g cooking apples,
  such as Bramleys
100g caster sugar,
  plus extra for dusting
finely grated zest and juice
  of half a lemon
150g blueberries
25g butter
1 egg, beaten
clotted cream or ice cream,
  for serving

passion fruit &
CUSTARD SOUFFLÉ

SERVES 4

Preheat the oven to 180°C/350°F/Gas mark 4. Grease four ramekins using half the butter. Dust the insides with 1 tbsp of the caster sugar.

Whisk the egg whites in a bowl until stiff, then add 1 tbsp of the caster sugar.

Scoop the passion fruit into the custard, and then gently fold in the whisked egg whites. Spoon the mixture into the prepared ramekins and place on a baking tray. Bake for 15–20 minutes.

While the soufflés are cooking, peel the bananas and then cut them in half lengthways.

Heat up a non-stick pan and add the remaining butter. When it's nut-brown in colour, add the remaining sugar and the halved bananas. Fry them on both sides until they are a nice golden colour, taking care not to break them up.

To serve, place the warm bananas on the plate, the soufflé on the side and, if you dare, a dollop of vanilla ice cream, too!

50g butter
3 tbsp caster sugar
4 medium egg whites
1 passion fruit, halved
8 tbsp fresh ready-made custard
2 medium bananas
vanilla ice cream (see page 146), to serve

The secret to foolproof dessert soufflés is to use ready-made custard, not the glow-in-the-dark, fluorescent type made by mixing powder with milk. Buy fresh, good-quality custard from a supermarket or good delicatessen.

spicy plum
CRUMBLE

SERVES 8

Preheat the oven to 200°C/400°F/Gas mark 6.

Sauté the plums with the butter in a hot frying pan for a few minutes. Add the split vanilla pod, star anise, nutmeg and cinnamon, red wine, syrup, sugar and water, then bring to the boil and simmer gently for 6–8 minutes.

As the plums break down to a thick, syrupy texture, put them in an ovenproof dish.

To make the crumble, mix the butter and flour together until the mixture resembles breadcrumbs, then mix in the sugar. Sprinkle the crumble over the plums and bake in the oven for 20–25 minutes, or until golden brown.

Remove from the oven and allow to cool slightly before serving with ice cream or double cream.

15 fresh dark plums,
   cut in half and
   stones removed
50g butter
1 vanilla pod, split
1 star anise
few gratings of nutmeg
2 cinnamon sticks
100ml red wine
5 tbsp golden syrup
4 tbsp caster sugar
50ml water

For the crumble
100g butter, softened
180–200g plain flour
100g demerara sugar

You can make crumble without cooking the filling simply by chopping apples and adding a few blackcurrants or something similar, putting the crumble mixture on top and baking in the oven for 25–30 minutes. This recipe is quicker, though, as the filling is already cooked when placed in the dish.

classic
SPOTTED DICK

SERVES 8

Butter a piece of greaseproof paper measuring about 60cm square with the soft butter.

Put all the dry ingredients in a bowl, then add the melted butter. Stir in the lemon juice and zest, egg and, while stirring slowly, add the milk and cream until you reach a dropping consistency.

Spoon the mixture onto the paper and roll up into a sausage shape about 6cm in diameter. Don't roll the paper too tight; otherwise the mixture will not rise and be light when cooked.

Tie at the ends with string and place the pudding in a hot steamer, fitted with a lid, and steam for about 1¼ hours until cooked.

Remove the pudding from the steamer and unwrap from the paper, then spoon into the bowls. Serve with custard (see page 23) or vanilla ice cream (see page 146).

25g soft butter, for greasing
350g plain flour
2 tbsp baking powder
150g shredded suet
75g caster sugar
150g currants
25g butter, melted
juice and zest of 2 lemons
1 egg
150ml milk
150ml double cream

Spotted dick is usually served with custard, but my grandmother served it with just plain butter while my auntie sprinkled demerara sugar over the top. The 'spotted' refers to the currants which resemble spots and the 'dick' actually comes from the word 'dough'. It's also known as spotted dog, plum bolster and spotted Richard.

baked parkin
WITH RHUBARB

Preheat the oven to 140°C/275°F/Gas mark 1. Grease a 30 x 20cm cake tin and line with greaseproof paper.

Sieve the flour, salt, ginger, nutmeg and mixed spice together into a large bowl. Mix in the oats.

Put the syrup, treacle, butter and soft brown sugar in a small saucepan and melt over a gentle heat, but do not boil. Stir into the flour mixture.

Mix in the beaten egg and milk to create a soft, almost pouring, consistency. Pour into the buttered tin.

Bake for 1–1¼ hours until firm in the centre. Remove from the oven and leave in the tin for 5–10 minutes before turning out.

Meanwhile, to make the hot spiced syrup, simply whisk all the ingredients together in a small pan and warm, but don't boil. Add the rhubarb and cook gently for 3–4 minutes to soften a little.

Serve the parkin warm, on top of the warm syrup and rhubarb and topped with ice cream. Drizzle over any remaining syrup and serve with a sprig of fresh mint.

170g self-raising flour
pinch of salt
3 tsp ground ginger
2 tsp nutmeg
1 tsp mixed spice
120g oat flakes
250g golden syrup
75g black treacle
150g unsalted butter,
    plus extra for greasing
150g soft dark brown sugar
2 medium eggs, beaten
25ml milk

For the syrup
200g golden syrup
100ml apple juice
1 tsp ground mixed spice
4 sticks fresh rhubarb,
    cut into 5cm lengths

To serve
vanilla ice cream (see page 146)
fresh mint

steamed treacle
SPONGE PUDDING

SERVES 6-8

Butter a 1.2-litre pudding basin well. Cut a double thickness of kitchen foil measuring approximately 30 x 40cm.

Grease a tablespoon and measure the 3 tbsp golden syrup into the pudding basin.

Sift the flour and baking powder into a large mixing bowl and add the soft butter, eggs, sugar and black treacle. Using an electric hand whisk (or a large fork and a lot of elbow grease), beat the mixture for about 2 minutes, or until it has thoroughly blended. Spoon the mixture into the basin and use the back of a spoon to level the top.

Cover the basin with the foil, making a pleat in the centre. Pull the foil down the outside of the basin and tie in place around the rim with string, taking the string over the top and tying it on the other side to make a handle for easy lifting. Trim off the excess foil all the way around.

Place the pudding in a steamer fitted over a saucepan of boiling water and steam the pudding for 2 hours, checking the water level halfway through.

To serve, loosen the pudding all around using a palette knife, invert it onto a warmed plate and pour the extra golden syrup over the top before taking it to the table. Serve with custard or ice cream.

3 tbsp golden syrup, plus 3-4 tbsp extra to serve
175g self-raising flour
1 rounded tsp baking powder
175g very soft butter
3 large eggs
175g soft light brown sugar
1 tbsp black treacle

fresh orange
CURD PUDDING

SERVES 4-6

Preheat the oven to 180°C/350°F/Gas mark 4. Butter the sides of
a 1-litre soufflé dish, or other similar ovenproof dish, and set aside.

Put the orange and lemon juices in a saucepan, bring to the boil and
boil until reduced by just over half. Set aside to cool.

In a bowl, beat the butter with the sugar and lemon zest until white
and creamy. Mix in the egg yolks, one at a time. Sift the flour and
baking powder together over the mixture, then mix to combine.

Slowly add the orange and lemon juice and milk to the mixture,
stirring to blend.

Now whisk the egg whites in another bowl until they form stiff peaks.
Beat a third of the whisked egg whites into the runny sponge mixture,
then carefully fold in the rest using a large spoon.

Stand the prepared dish in a roasting tin, then pour in the mixture.
Pour boiling water around the dish to create a bain-marie and place
in the oven.

Bake for 50–60 minutes until the pudding is golden brown and firm
on top. Cover the dish with foil if the top browns too quickly.

Remove the dish from the oven and dust the pudding with icing sugar
before serving.

60g butter, softened, plus extra
    for greasing
300ml fresh orange juice
grated zest and juice of 1 lemon
90g caster sugar
4 large eggs, separated
70g self-raising flour
½ tsp baking powder
160ml milk
icing sugar, for dusting

sticky toffee pudding
WITH TOFFEE SAUCE

SERVES 6-8

Preheat the oven to 200°C/400°F/Gas mark 6. Grease a 23cm tin thoroughly with 25g of the butter, then dust the inside of the tin with flour.

Using a food mixer, blend the remaining butter and sugar together. Slowly add the golden syrup, treacle, eggs and vanilla extract to the butter mixture and continue mixing. Turn the mixer down to a slow speed and then add the flour. Once all the ingredients are combined, turn off the mixer.

Put the dates in a saucepan with the water and bring to the boil. Purée the water and date mixture and add the bicarbonate of soda. While it is still hot, quickly add this mixture to the egg mix. Once the mixture is combined, pour into the prepared tin and bake for 40–45 minutes until the top is just firm to the touch.

Remove the pudding from the oven and allow it to cool, then turn out of the tin and cut into squares.

To make the sauce, melt the butter and sugar together in a small pan, add the cream and bring to the boil. Simmer for a few minutes until the sauce reaches the desired consistency.

To serve, reheat the sponge in a microwave or heat for 5 minutes in the oven at 180°C/350°F/Gas mark 4. Place onto a plate with lots of the sauce on the top and a scoop of vanilla ice cream if you wish.

The sponge and sauce can be made in advance. The sponge can even be frozen and both can be plated up and reheated in the microwave.

75g soft butter
200g self-raising flour, plus extra
    for dusting
175g dark brown demerara sugar
1 tbsp golden syrup
2 tbsp black treacle
2 eggs
1 tsp vanilla extract
200g pitted dried dates
300ml water
1 tsp bicarbonate of soda

For the toffee sauce
100g dark soft sugar
100g butter
200ml double cream

hot chocolate fondants
WITH BERRIES & MINT

SERVES 6

Preheat the oven to 180°C/350°F/Gas mark 4.

Finely grate 40g of the chocolate. Rub half the butter all over the inside of six tall dariole moulds (or similar containers). Dust well with the grated chocolate, shaking out any excess. Set aside on a baking tray.

Melt the remaining chocolate (including any shaken-out excess) and butter in a small heatproof bowl over a pan of barely simmering water, or in a microwave-proof bowl in the microwave on full power for 2–3 minutes, stirring once. Do not overheat or the chocolate will 'seize', or turn solid. Scrape this mixture into a bigger bowl, then beat in the ground almonds, egg yolks and cornflour.

Whisk the egg whites in a separate bowl until they form stiff but not dry peaks. Gradually beat in the caster sugar – you may prefer to use a hand-held electric whisk for this.

Fold the meringue mixture into the melted chocolate mixture. Spoon half the combined mixture into the base of the mould, place a chocolate truffle on top, then fill each mould with the remaining mixture. Smooth the tops of the fondants.

Bake the fondants in the oven for 10–15 minutes until risen and slightly wobbly (they're best eaten as soon as they're cooked).

To make the mint froth, bring the milk to a boil, remove from the heat, add the crème de menthe, then 'froth' with a hand blender. Turn the fondants out onto plates and serve with fresh berries and mint froth.

190g dark chocolate with at least 60% cocoa solids
100g butter, softened
35g ground almonds
2 large eggs, separated
35g cornflour
85g caster sugar
6 plain chocolate truffles
strawberries, raspberries and blueberries, to decorate

For the mint froth
150ml full-fat milk
1 tbsp crème de menthe

fig
FRITTERS

SERVES 8

Heat 7.5cm of oil in a deep, heavy pot to 180°C/350°F.

Wipe the figs with a damp cloth to remove any dust.

To make the batter, combine all the ingredients in a large bowl and whisk until just blended; don't worry if there are a few lumps.

Dip two figs into the batter and immediately deep-fry for about 2 minutes until golden brown. Using a wire-mesh skimmer or slotted metal spoon, carefully transfer to paper towels to drain. Repeat with the remaining figs.

To serve, put a small scoop of vanilla ice cream in the centre of each bowl with a whole fig. Dust with caster sugar and sprinkle the crystallized ginger on the ice cream.

vegetable or sunflower oil,
for deep-frying
8 large ripe figs

For the fritter batter
125g plain flour
125g rice flour
170g sugar
pinch of salt
1 egg
250ml ice-cold water

To serve
500ml vanilla ice cream
(see page 146)
50g julienned crystallized ginger
caster sugar, for sprinkling

A great dessert for when you don't want the fuss of making something beforehand. Simply fry the figs in batter at the last minute. While the figs are frying, scoop the ice cream into bowls, then add the drained fig fritters to the side, sprinkle with a little sugar and you're done.

mincemeat &
APPLE JALOUSIE

SERVES 8

Preheat the oven to 200°C/400°F/Gas mark 6. Lightly grease a large, solid baking tray.

Put the mincemeat in a large bowl, then add the apple, orange zest, spice and rum and give it a good mix.

Unroll the pastry onto a surface lightly dusted with flour, and roll it into two slightly thinner rectangles, each measuring approximately 15 x 45cm.

Roll one of the pieces of pastry a little thinner and larger, then fold it in half lengthways. Using a sharp knife, cut diagonally about 5cm into the fold at 2.5cm intervals.

Place the second rectangle of pastry on the baking tray and pile the mincemeat filling onto the pastry, leaving a 2.5cm edge all around. Brush the edge with a little cold water.

Unfold the first rectangle of pastry and place it over the mincemeat. Using your thumbs, press the edges all around the filling to seal them. Finally, trim the pastry to 1cm around the filling and either crimp the edges with your fingers or use a knife.

Brush all over with the beaten egg, then sprinkle the sugar and cinnamon mixture over the top. Bake for 30–35 minutes and sprinkle with the icing sugar just before serving with cream or custard or, as my gran used to have it, with ice cream.

400g mincemeat
1 small Bramley cooking apple
   (225g), peeled, cored and
   finely chopped
zest of 1 orange
½ tsp ground mixed spice
2 tbsp rum
375g simple rough puff pastry
   (see page 13)
   or packet of fresh ready-rolled,
   all-butter puff pastry
plain flour, for dusting
1 large egg, lightly beaten
1 dsp golden granulated sugar,
   mixed with ¼ tsp
   ground cinnamon
icing sugar, for dusting

kentish
PUDDING PIE

SERVES 6

Make the pastry following the instructions on page 12.

Preheat the oven to 200°C/400°F/Gas Mark 6. Line six 9cm tart tins with the pastry and blind-bake for 10–12 minutes. Remove from the oven and cool slightly.

Place the eggs and sugar into a bowl and whisk to combine.

Place the cream and milk into a saucepan and bring to a boil. Pour onto the eggs and sugar and whisk. Return to the saucepan and bring to a boil, stirring constantly. Cook until just thickened, then remove from the heat.

Whisk in the ground rice, nutmeg and lemon zest and juice. Pour into the tart cases. Sprinkle the currants over the custard.

Place the tarts onto a baking tray and bake for 10 minutes until just set and lightly golden. Serve with the roasted crab apples (see below), junket ice cream and a dusting of icing sugar.

500g rich shortcrust pastry
  (see page 12)
2 eggs
75g caster sugar
150ml double cream
250ml milk
100g ground rice
pinch nutmeg
zest and juice of 1½ lemons
125g currants
icing sugar, to serve

To serve
junket ice cream (see page 150)
roasted crab apples (see below)

The perfect accompaniment to the sweetness of this pie is the strong, sharp and bitter taste of roasted crab apples. Simply heat 500g crab apples with 50g butter for 3–4 minutes and then toss into a roasting tray with 2 cinnamon sticks, 1 tsp ground cinnamon and 75g caster sugar. Leave for 4–6 minutes until just tender. Serve with a dusting of icing sugar and a dollop of junket ice cream to finish.

slow-roasted peaches
WITH ORANGE SAUCE

SERVES 6

First, make the orange sauce. Put the sugar in a heavy-based saucepan with the water and dissolve over a low heat. When the sugar syrup is completely clear, increase the heat and cook for about 5 minutes to a light caramel.

Remove from the heat and carefully stir in the orange juice (it will splutter). Slit open the vanilla pod, scrape out the seeds and add these to the orange caramel sauce. Set aside to cool until thickened, then stir in the pistachio nuts and whole almonds.

Preheat the oven to 170°C/340°F/Gas mark 3½.

Using a blowtorch, blacken the peach skins, then use a clean cloth to wipe the skins away.

Brush the peaches liberally with the butter using a pastry brush. Sprinkle them with the sugar, making sure they are thoroughly coated (you can also put the sugar on a plate and roll the peaches in it).

Place the peaches in a small roasting tin and spoon the orange sauce over them. Roast, uncovered, in the oven for about 30 minutes until the peaches are softened but still whole, basting them with the pan juices every 10 minutes or so. Add the raspberries to the roasting tin for the final 10 minutes.

Remove from the oven, cover the tin loosely with foil and leave to cool – this encourages juices to gather in the bottom of the tin.

Serve the peaches with the orange sauce spooned over and the almond ice cream on the side.

6 medium white peaches
50g unsalted butter, softened
  until runny but not melted
100g caster sugar
150g fresh raspberries
vanilla ice cream (see page 146),
  for serving

For the orange sauce
150g caster sugar
3 tbsp water
250ml fresh orange juice
1 vanilla pod
100g pistachio nuts, shelled
75g whole almonds
almond ice cream (see page 146,
  bottom), for serving

cold PUDDINGS

delice
AU CASSIS

SERVES 8-10

Put all syrup ingredients in a pan and bring to the boil; stir occasionally. Boil for about 3 minutes, skimming the surface if necessary. Pass the syrup through a conical strainer and leave until cold before using.

Purée the blackcurrants in the blender with 50ml syrup, then pass the purée through a conical strainer. Soak 4½ gelatine leaves in cold water for 15 minutes, then drain. Reserve 4 tbsp blackcurrant purée and put the rest in a saucepan with the powdered milk and vanilla pod; bring to the boil. Whisk the yolks and sugar in a bowl until they form a ribbon. Pour the boiling purée onto the egg mixture, whisking continuously, then pour back into the pan over a low heat, stirring constantly with a spatula until the mousse coats the spatula. Do not boil. Remove from the heat and stir the drained gelatine into the mousse. Discard the vanilla, then strain the mousse into a bowl and leave to cool, stirring occasionally to prevent a skin from forming.

Place the sponge flan on a serving plate. Mix 50ml syrup and 1 tbsp purée and brush over the sponge. Place a 25cm flan ring, 6cm deep, onto the sponge and cut around to make the base.

When the mousse is lukewarm, gently fold in the meringue, then the crème de cassis, using a balloon whisk. Beat the double cream until it forms a ribbon. Using a spatula, gently fold into the mixture, and assemble the dessert immediately, before the mousse sets. Fill the flan ring with mousse, leaving a 3mm gap at the top. Smooth the surface with a palette knife. Put in a freezer or very cold fridge for several hours.

Soak the remaining gelatine in cold water for 15 minutes, then drain well. Mix 50ml syrup with the remaining purée and stir in the gelatine. Pass through a muslin cloth into a jug, then glaze the top of the dessert. Leave to set in the fridge. To remove the ring, heat the outside with a blowtorch for a few seconds, then slide it up. Decorate with fruit to serve.

350g blackcurrants
150ml syrup, divided into
   3 equal quantities (see below)
7½ gelatine leaves
12g powdered milk
½ vanilla pod
3 medium egg yolks
25g sugar
25cm ready-made sponge flan
200ml crème de cassis
1 quantity Italian meringue
   (made with 3 egg whites,
   180g sugar, 5 tbsp water;
   see page 21)
400ml double cream
blackcurrants, raspberries,
   strawberries, blackberries and
   a mint sprig, for decorating

For the syrup
375g sugar
325ml water
30g glucose
(any leftover syrup can be stored
   in the fridge)

puff pastry &
RASPBERRY STACK

Preheat the oven to 220°C/425°F/Gas mark 7.

Cut the puff pastry into circles with a diameter of 7.5cm. Place on a non-stick oven tray and leave to rest in the fridge for 10 minutes.

Turn the pastry over (this will ensure an even rise when baked) and dust with icing sugar. Bake in the top of the oven for 5–6 minutes. Remove from the oven and allow to cool, then carefully slice each pastry into three discs (top/middle/bottom).

To make the sauce, blend half the raspberries with 1 tbsp of the icing sugar and a little water and pass through a sieve.

Beat the cream, mascarpone and remaining sugar together.

Place a spoonful of the mascarpone mixture on top of one of the discs (the base disc) and top with a couple of halved strawberries. Place the raspberries around the edge, then top with another disc (the middle disc) of pastry and repeat the process. To finish, top with a final piece of pastry (the top disc).

Spoon the sauce onto a serving plate and place the puff pastry stack in the centre. Dust with icing sugar and serve with a sugar twist if you wish.

300g ready-rolled puff pastry
45g icing sugar, plus extra
    for dusting
400g fresh raspberries
75ml double cream
175g mascarpone cheese
50g fresh strawberries
spun sugar, optional
    (see pages 18–19)

ginger & syrup
CHEESECAKE

SERVES 2

Crush the biscuits and mix with the softened butter. Place two 5cm metal rings on serving plates and fill with the crumb mixture to form the base of the cheesecake.

Place the cream cheese in a bowl with the diced ginger and about 4 tbsp of the syrup and mix well. Spoon the mixture into the rings and level the top.

Top each cheesecake with the grated chocolate. Slice the remaining ginger in half and arrange on the top of the cheesecakes.

Place a warm cloth around the rings to loosen the cheesecakes, or briefly warm with a blowtorch, and carefully lift the rings off. Garnish with a sugar twist and serve.

4 digestive biscuits
15g butter, softened
300g full-fat cream cheese
4 pieces of ginger in syrup,
  2 diced
3 tbsp grated dark chocolate
2 quantities of spun sugar,
  optional (see pages 18-19)

lemon curd
SYLLABUB

SERVES 4

Crumble the shortbread into the bottom of four wine glasses and moisten with half the wine.

Mix the mascarpone and cream with the sugar. When it reaches soft peaks, fold in the remaining wine and swirl in the lemon curd, leaving a marbling of yellow through the cream.

Spoon the mixture into the glasses, top with a spoonful of double cream and scatter with the toasted almonds. Garnish with a sprig of mint and serve.

4 shortbread biscuits (or lemon-flavoured shortbread)
50ml white wine
75g mascarpone cheese
250ml double cream, plus extra for serving
4 tbsp icing sugar
8 tbsp lemon curd
2 tbsp flaked almonds, toasted
fresh mint sprigs

The secret of this syllabub is to make it quickly and use good-quality lemon curd. It should be served in the summertime, following a light main course, such as poached salmon – the two flavours work well together.

black forest
GATEAU

SERVES 8-10

Preheat the oven to 180°C/350°F/Gas mark 4. Grease and line a deep 26cm springform cake tin.

Break the eggs into a mixing bowl, add the sugar and whisk well until the ribbon stage, or very light and fluffy. Carefully fold in the sifted flour and cocoa powder.

Pour the mix into the prepared tin and bake for about 55 minutes, or until cooked. Turn out onto a wire rack and leave to cool.

Drain the cherries, reserving the juice. Put the juice into a pan and bring to the boil. While the juice is heating, mix the arrowroot with a little water in a small bowl, to slacken to a paste. When the cherry juice is boiling, mix the arrowroot paste into it. Strain through a sieve over the cherries with the Kirsch and leave to one side to cool.

Slice the sponge into three layers using a sharp knife. Sandwich the three layers together using the whipped cream and half the cherries and almonds.

Melt the chocolate in a bowl over a pan of simmering water. Add the peppermint essence and sugar, stir and spread onto a tray lined with cling film. Place in the fridge to set.

When the chocolate is set, break it into large shards and stick randomly around the edge of the cake (if necessary, place a blob of cream on the back of the shards to help them stay in place).

Top with the remaining cherries and serve.

For the sponge
butter, for greasing
9 eggs
250g caster sugar
215g self-raising flour, sifted
40g cocoa powder

For the filling and topping
1 x 340g jar of cherries
   (drained weight)
2 tbsp arrowroot
a good dash of kirsch
750ml double cream, whipped
50g flaked almonds, toasted

For the chocolate shards
300g dark chocolate
½ tsp peppermint essence
110g demerara sugar

quick strawberry
& VANILLA GATEAU

SERVES 6-8

Using a 20–25cm stainless-steel ring, cut out the centre of the flan. With a sharp knife, slice the disc in half through the middle so you end up with two thin discs.

Whip the double cream with 25g of the caster sugar, the vanilla seeds and a shot of Drambuie to a thick peak consistency. Fold in the custard, then chill in the fridge.

Set aside 10 whole, small strawberries for the garnish. Cut the green top from all the remaining strawberries and cut them in half lengthways.

Place one sponge disk in the bottom of the ring, then line the ring with the largest strawberry halves, cut-side against the ring. You won't need all of the strawberries so save the remainder for the topping. Place the whipped cream in the ring and gently spread to the edges. Add the rest of the strawberries and smooth the top.

Place the remaining disc of sponge on top, lift the cake onto a plate and remove the ring by carefully warming the edges with a hot cloth and lifting it straight off.

Put the remaining caster sugar into a very clean pan and heat gently until it caramelizes, then remove from the heat and leave to cool slightly.

While this is cooling, take a metal skewer that has been heated until red-hot and score the top of the gâteau in lines to create a diamond pattern. Once cooled, the caramelised sugar should be made into spun sugar (see pages 18-19) and placed on top of the dish. Dress the top with the remaining strawberries and the berries, sprinkle over the sieved icing sugar and garnish with sprigs of fresh mint.

1 large ready-made flan case
750ml double cream
100g caster sugar
1 vanilla pod, seeds only
1 shot of Drambuie
200ml ready-made custard
1 punnet of small strawberries
1½ punnets of large strawberries
1 punnet of mixed berries,
   such as redcurrants,
   blueberries and blackberries
50g icing sugar
fresh mint sprigs

baked chocolate mousse
WITH CANDIED FENNEL

Preheat the oven to 180°C/350°F/Gas mark 4. Line the base and sides of a 20cm spring-bottomed cake tin with greaseproof paper and add the slices of fennel onto the base.

Melt the chocolate and butter in a metal bowl placed over a pan of simmering water.

Whisk the egg yolks with 2 tbsp of the sugar for 30 seconds. Stir in the melted chocolate and mix well.

Beat the egg whites with the remaining sugar until very stiff, then quickly fold one-third of the whites into the chocolate mix. Gently fold in the remainder and pour the mix into the cake tin.

Place on the middle shelf of the oven and bake for 20 minutes. Remove from the oven and allow to cool before serving.

To make the candied fennel, slice the fennel bulb and add to a pan with the sugar and the water. Bring to the boil and simmer for 20–30 minutes and allow to cool.

Serve in a wedge with some of the fennel and juices and a spoonful of whipped cream.

½ fennel bulb, thinly sliced
300g dark bitter chocolate
   (minimum 60% cocoa fat)
150g unsalted butter
6 eggs, separated
50g caster sugar
150ml whipped double cream,
   to serve

For the candied fennel
1 fennel bulb
100g caster sugar
100ml water

profiteroles
SERVES 4-6

Preheat the oven to 200°C/400°F/Gas mark 6. Lightly oil a large baking tray. To make the pastry, put the butter and sugar into a large pan with the water. Place over a low heat to melt, then increase the heat and shoot in the flour and salt all at once.

Remove from the heat and quickly beat the mixture vigorously until a smooth paste forms. Replace the pan over the heat and stir with a spatula for 1 minute. Immediately add the eggs, off the heat, one at a time, mixing with a spatula. Continue beating until the paste is smooth and glossy, with a soft dropping consistency. The mixture will be shiny and smooth and fall from a spoon if given a sharp tap.

Dip a teaspoon into some warm water and lift out a spoon of the profiterole mixture. Rub the top of the mixture with a wet finger to get rid of any bumps and spoon onto the baking tray. Place in the oven, throw in half a cup of water into the bottom of the oven and shut the door quickly. This will make more steam to help the pastry rise better. Bake for 25–30 minutes, until golden brown (if too pale they'll become soggy when cool). Remove from the oven and prick the base of each profiterole. Place on the baking tray with the holes facing upwards and return to the oven for 5 minutes where the warm air helps to dry out the centres.

For the filling, lightly whip the cream with the zest until soft peaks form. Do not over-whip. When the profiteroles are cold, use a piping bag with a plain 5mm nozzle to pipe the cream into the holes of the profiteroles.

For the sauce, melt the chocolate in a bowl over a pan of simmering water. Put the sugar in a small pan with the water and bring to the boil. Stir the melted chocolate, then add the water and sugar mixture and stir until smooth and shiny. Arrange the buns on a serving dish and pour over the hot sauce. Eat hot or cold.

For the choux pastry
85g unsalted butter
4 tsp caster sugar
200ml cold water
115g plain flour
pinch of salt
3 medium eggs, beaten

For the cream filling
600ml double cream
zest of 3 oranges

For the chocolate sauce
175g good-quality plain
    chocolate, broken into pieces
50g caster sugar
100ml water

figs in
VANILLA SYRUP

MAKES 500G

Preheat the oven to 150°C/300°F/Gas mark 2.

Place the figs in a warmed ovenproof jar with the cut sides facing outwards. Pack the centre of the jar tightly with figs and put two halves, cut-side uppermost, in the top of the jar.

Put the sugar, vanilla pod and cinnamon stick into a saucepan with the water. Slowly bring to the boil and heat, stirring continuously until the sugar has completely dissolved. Boil for 1 minute, then remove from the heat.

Lift the vanilla pod out of the syrup. Using a small knife, scrape the black seeds into the syrup and stir in the citric acid. Remove the cinnamon stick. Tuck the vanilla pod down the side of the jar.

Pour the syrup over the figs to cover completely and come almost to the brim of the jar. Cover the top of the jar with a piece of foil. Stand the jar on a baking tray lined with several sheets of folded newspaper and bake in the preheated oven for 20–30 minutes until the syrup has turned a delicate pink and the figs are just beginning to rise in the jar.

Using oven gloves or a cloth, transfer the jar to a wooden board, close the lid fully and leave to cool completely. When cold, check that the jar is properly sealed. Label and store in a cool, dark place. The figs will keep for 6–12 months.

8–9 firm fresh figs, halved
100g caster sugar
½ vanilla pod, split lengthways
½ cinnamon stick
400ml water
½ tsp citric acid

petits
MONTS BLANCS

SERVES 8

Preheat the oven to 150°C/300°F/Gas mark 2. Line a baking tray with baking parchment or a non-stick cooking mat.

To make the meringue, put the egg whites in a large clean bowl and, using an electric whisk on a low speed, begin whisking. Continue for about 2 minutes until the whites are foamy, then switch the speed to medium and carry on whisking until the egg whites reach the stiff-peak stage. Next, whisk the sugar in on high, a dessertspoon at a time, until you have a stiff and glossy mixture.

Spoon 8 heaped dessertspoons of the mixture onto the baking tray, spacing them evenly. Using the back of the spoon or a small palette knife, hollow out the centres.

Place on the centre shelf of the oven, immediately reduce the heat to 140°C/275°F/Gas mark 1 and leave them for 30 minutes. After that, turn the oven off and leave the meringues to dry out in the warmth of the oven until the oven is completely cold (usually about 4 hours or overnight). The meringues will store well in a tin or plastic box, and will even freeze extremely well.

To assemble the Monts Blancs, spoon equal quantities of the crème de marrons into each meringue.

Whisk all the ingredients (except the icing sugar) for the mascarpone cream together, then spoon equal amounts on top of the chestnut purée. A light dusting of icing sugar helps them resemble the snowcapped mountain they are named after.

For the meringue
2 large egg whites
110g white caster sugar

For the filling
2 x 250g tins crème de marrons
    de l'Ardèche, chilled

For the mascarpone cream
250g mascarpone cheese
200ml fromage frais
1 rounded dsp caster sugar
1 tsp pure vanilla extract
a little icing sugar, for dusting

baked chocolate &
ORANGE CHEESECAKE

SERVES 8-10

Preheat the oven to 180°C/350°F/Gas mark 4. Butter a 23cm springform cake tin.

Cut the sponge horizontally into two discs. Use one to line the cake tin. Drizzle with 1 tbsp Grand Marnier.

Mix together the sugar, orange zest and juice and cornflour in a bowl using a wooden spoon, then use an electric hand mixer to beat in the cream cheese. Add the eggs one by one, beating constantly until all the eggs are well incorporated.

Slice open the vanilla pod, remove the seeds with a sharp knife and place the seeds into the cream-cheese mixture, add 2 tbsp of Grand Marnier, if using, and mix everything together well. Add the cream and beat well until the mixture is smooth.

Pour half of the mixture gently over the sponge base in the cake tin. Top with half of the chocolate pieces and smooth over with a stepped palette knife. Repeat. Sit the tin in a baking tray filled with 2–3mm of warm water to help create steam during cooking. Place in the oven and bake for 50 minutes until the top is golden. Remove from the oven and leave to cool and set completely before removing from the tin.

Meanwhile, melt the white and dark chocolate separately in bowls over simmering water. Cover a baking tray tightly in cling film. Pour the dark chocolate and the white chocolate onto the tray. Using your finger, swirl the two chocolates together to create a marble effect. Chill to set.

Serve the cheesecake cut into wedges, with a piece of the marbled chocolate and a drizzle of cream.

butter, for greasing
23cm sponge (cut from a large
    bought flan case)
3 tbsp Grand Marnier
200g caster sugar
zest of 2 oranges
juice of 1 orange
4 level tbsp cornflour
850g full-fat soft cream cheese
3 medium eggs
1 vanilla pod
375ml double cream, plus extra
    for serving
36 dark chocolate pieces

For the marbled chocolate
150g white chocolate
150g dark chocolate

crème CARAMEL

Preheat the oven to 140°C/275°F/Gas mark 1.

First, make the caramel. Put the sugar in a saucepan over a high heat. When the sugar begins to melt, cook until it has become a uniform syrup about two or three shades darker than golden syrup.

Take the pan off the heat and carefully add the water – it will splutter and bubble a bit but will soon stop. Stir and when the syrup is smooth once again, quickly pour it into the base of six ramekins, tipping them around to coat the sides a little.

Pour the milk and cream into another pan and leave it to heat gently while you whisk together the eggs, sugar and vanilla seeds in a large bowl. When the milk and cream are steaming hot, pour onto the egg and sugar mixture, whisking thoroughly until blended. Pour the liquid into the ramekins.

Place the ramekins in a large roasting tray. Transfer the tray carefully to the oven, then pour hot water into it to come two-thirds of the way up the sides of the ramekins. Bake for 45–60 minutes.

Cool and chill the crème caramel. Remove from the fridge 1 hour before you are ready to serve them. Free the edges by running a knife around before inverting them onto serving plates.

150ml milk
275ml double cream
4 large eggs
40g caster sugar
1 vanilla pod, seeds only

For the caramel
110g caster sugar
2 tbsp hot tap water

raspberry & NOUGAT SEMIFREDDO

SERVES 8

Grease a small loaf tin with olive oil, then line with cling film.

Separate the egg yolks and the whites into two bowls.

Add the sugar to the egg yolks and whisk until frothy. Add the mascarpone and keep mixing, then fold in the chopped nougat.

Whip up the egg whites, then carefully fold them into the mixed yolks with the raspberries.

Pour the mixture into the lined tin and freeze it until it is firmly set (preferably overnight).

To serve, tip the semifreddo out of the mould onto a serving plate. Serve a slice of the semifreddo with some raspberries and a doughnut and with a little raspberry sauce drizzled over the top.

olive oil, for greasing
4 eggs
6 tbsp caster sugar
400g mascarpone cheese
100g nougat with pistachio
    nuts, chopped
200g raspberries

To serve
fresh raspberries
8 fresh doughnuts
raspberry sauce (see page 22)

Semifreddo in Italian translates to 'half-cold'. This is a standard recipe that you can vary: for instance, using strawberries instead of raspberries. Omit the nougat if you wish. The recipe works well with pistachios and hazelnuts and also fruit such as lemon – lemon and vodka semifreddo with hazelnuts is fantastic.

vanilla panna cotta
WITH BALSAMIC BERRIES
SERVES 6-8

Soak the gelatine in the milk and leave to one side.

Put the orange zest, vanilla pods and caster sugar in a pan. Add 800ml of the cream and bring to the boil. Simmer until the mixture is reduced by a third.

While the cream is reducing, remove the gelatine from the milk and pour the milk in a pan to warm gently. When it is warm, add the soaked gelatine and stir to dissolve. Add to the warm cream, pass through a sieve and leave to cool.

Lightly whip the remaining cream and fold into the setting mixture, together with the vodka. Pour the mixture into 6–8 dariole moulds, ramekins or similar-sized moulds and place in the fridge to set.

While the panna cotta is setting, make the balsamic berries. Put the strawberries, raspberries, blueberries, balsamic vinegar and sugar into a large bowl and toss well. Allow to marinate for 2–3 hours, tossing occasionally.

Remove the panna cotta from the fridge and slide a knife around the edge to loosen. Alternatively, dip the moulds very briefly in hot water to loosen the panna cotta. Tip them out into the middle of the plates and spoon the balsamic berries around the edge.

4 leaves of gelatine
120ml milk
zest of 2 oranges
2 vanilla pods, split
150g caster sugar
1.2 litres double cream
80ml vodka

For the balsamic berries
200g strawberries, hulled
150g raspberries
100g blueberries
75ml good-quality aged
    balsamic vinegar
25g caster sugar

raspberry-vodka terrine
WITH LIME SAUCE

SERVES 10

Make the jelly by bringing the sugar and water to the boil. Meanwhile, soak the gelatine in a little cold water. When the water has boiled, re-measure the mixture to ensure it makes up 1 litre (any excess can be used for the sauce). Add the squeezed-out gelatine to the pan and mix gently. Pass through a sieve into a bowl and allow to cool until it is just starting to thicken.

Line a terrine mould first with olive oil and then with cling film. Pour the vodka into the setting syrup. Spoon a little of the jelly into the base of the terrine and allow it to start to set. Layer the raspberries with a little of the jelly to set each layer. Allow to set.

To make the sauce, put the sugar and lime juice in a pan with 150ml water and bring to a simmer. Dissolve the arrowroot in a little water and, using a whisk, mix it into the pan little by little until you have a sauce consistency. Pass through a sieve, add the zest and allow to cool.

Turn the terrine out of the mould onto a serving plate and remove the cling film. Serve the sauce separately.

450g caster sugar
1 litre water
8 gelatine leaves
olive oil, for greasing
70–100ml vodka, to taste
3 x 225g punnets of raspberries

For the sauce
150g caster sugar
150ml water
zest and juice of 5 limes
1 tsp arrowroot

Using arrowroot keeps the sauce clear; cornflour will create a cloudy sauce. You can mix and match the fruit with this recipe – try layers of mango raspberries, strawberries and blueberries. Pineapple doesn't work, though; it contains an acid that causes the jelly to dissolve.

clotted cream
SUMMER PUDDING
SERVES 4

Put half the frozen fruit in a blender and whiz to purée it well. Add some sugar to taste.

Line four small moulds or small pudding basins with cling film. Remove the crusts from the bread and cut circles to fit the base of the moulds. Dip one side of the bread circles into the puréed fruit and use to line the base of each mould, dipped-side facing out. Line the sides of the moulds with more dipped bread, dipped-side out.

Half-fill the centre of each mould with some of the defrosted whole fruit, then add a teaspoon of clotted cream. Top with the remaining defrosted fruit and some of the juices, then top with another circle of dipped bread. Chill the puddings in the fridge for at least 30 minutes before serving.

To serve, tip the puddings out from the moulds onto serving plates. Pour over the remaining puréed sauce, scatter the fruit around the pudding and dust with icing sugar.

400g mixed frozen
   fruit, defrosted
50g icing sugar, plus extra
   for dusting
10 slices white bread
1 small tub clotted cream
1 punnet each of strawberries,
   blueberries, raspberries
   and redcurrants

strawberry
JELLY

SERVES 4-6

Slice 500g of the strawberries and place in a large heatproof bowl set over a pan of gently simmering water. Stir in the sugar and lemon juice. Cover the bowl with cling film and leave for 30–40 minutes, checking the water in the pan occasionally and topping up with boiling water as necessary. The fruit will yield a clear, pink, fragrant juice.

Meanwhile, line a large sieve with wet muslin and place over a clean bowl. Pour the strawberry juice into the sieve and leave it to drip through, but don't rub the pulp; otherwise the juice will lose its clarity. Discard the fruit pulp.

Soften the gelatine sheets in cold water. Meanwhile, pour the strawberry juice into a clean pan and heat until on the point of boiling, then take off the heat. Remove the gelatine from the cold water, squeezing out any excess water and then slip the gelatine into the hot juice, whisking until dissolved. Pass through a sieve into a bowl.

Allow to cool, then mix in the water and crème de pêche. Leave until the jelly is cold and just on the point of setting. Meanwhile, place 4–6 wine glasses in the fridge and allow to chill.

Slice the remaining strawberries. Dip the slices quickly into a little of the setting jelly and stick to the inside of the chilled wine glasses.

Now for the fun bit. To make this jelly sparkle, whisk the setting jelly until lightly frothy and divide it among the glasses. Chill until completely set.

To serve, top with a thin float of double cream and a spoonful of whipped cream – keep it simple.

600g strawberries, hulled
100g caster sugar
juice of 1 lemon
8 sheets of leaf gelatine
75ml water
2 tbsp crème de pêche
double cream and whipped
   cream, to serve

raspberry &
PASSION FRUIT PAVLOVA

SERVES 4-6

Preheat the oven to 140°C/275°F/Gas mark 1. Cover a large baking tray with non-stick baking parchment.

Take the made-up meringue and fold in the cornflour and vinegar. Spoon the mixture onto the baking tray and spread into a large nest shape (or 10 small ones).

Place in the oven and cook for 10 minutes, then turn the heat down to its lowest setting for a few hours or leave overnight.

To serve, whip the cream into soft peaks. Cut open the passion fruit and spoon the insides into a bowl. Brush the melted white chocolate into the centre of the meringue and fill with the whipped cream.

Sprinkle over the fresh raspberries, then spoon over the passion-fruit pulp. Top with fresh sprigs of mint and serve.

1 quantity cold meringue
  (see page 20)
2 tsp cornflour
1 tsp white-wine vinegar
250ml double cream
5 passion fruit
150g white chocolate, melted
500g fresh raspberries
mint sprigs

The cornflour and white-wine vinegar listed in the ingredients are what give this meringue that wonderfully gooey texture.

raspberry
MARSHMALLOWS

MAKES ABOUT 450G

Put the granulated sugar, glucose and water in a heavy-based saucepan. Bring to the boil and continue cooking until it reaches 127°C/260°F on a sugar thermometer.

Meanwhile, soak the gelatine in 140ml cold water. Beat the egg whites until stiff. When the syrup is up to temperature, carefully slide in the softened gelatine sheets and their soaking water. The syrup will bubble up, so take care not to burn yourself. Pour the syrup into a metal jug.

Continue to beat the egg whites (preferably with an electric whisk) while pouring in the hot syrup from the jug. The mixture will become shiny and start to thicken. Add the vanilla extract and continue whisking for about 5–10 minutes, until the mixture is stiff and thick enough to hold its shape on the whisk.

Lightly oil a shallow 30 x 20cm baking tray. Dust it with sieved icing sugar and cornflour, then spoon half the mixture over and smooth it with a wet palette knife if necessary.

Roughly break the raspberries in half and spread over the marshmallow, then top with the remaining marshmallow. Leave to set in the fridge for at least 1 hour.

Dust the work surface with more icing sugar and cornflour. Loosen the marshmallow around the sides of the tray with a palette knife, then turn it out onto the dusted surface. Cut into squares and roll in the sugar and cornflour. Leave to dry a little on a wire rack, then pack into an airtight box.

455g granulated sugar
1 tbsp liquid glucose
200ml water
9 sheets of gelatine
2 large egg whites
1 tsp vanilla extract
oil, for greasing
125g fresh raspberries, coated in icing sugar or cornflour
icing sugar, for dusting
cornflour, for dusting

membrello

SERVES 12-14

Put the sugar and water in a saucepan set over a gentle heat. Add the grated quince and bring to a boil, then turn down to a simmer and cook, uncovered, for 2 hours, stirring occasionally until the liquid has thickened and comes away from the sides of the pan when stirred.

Remove from the heat, allow to cool slightly, then pour into a tin or mould lined with cling film.

Refrigerate for at least 2 hours before unwrapping and serving with cheese and biscuits. Membrello will keep for a few months.

1kg preserving sugar
700ml water
1kg quince, peeled, cored
  and grated

This recipe is also known as quince cheese. Quinces, like apples, produce a natural pectin, making them ideal for jellying, and this Spanish recipe is a set jelly. The fruit originally comes from Turkey and Iran and is almost a cross between a pear and an apple – rather like like a fat pear. Peeled and then mixed to create this fantastic jelly, it tastes superb. Serve on its own, in an apple tart, apple pie or with some cheese such as Stilton.

tarts &
FLANS

apple & thyme
TARTE TATIN

SERVES 4-6

Preheat the oven to 200°C/400°F/Gas mark 6.

To make the caramel, put the sugar into a 20cm ovenproof pan and heat gently without stirring until it turns golden brown. Remove from the heat, add the butter and stir in gently.

Roll out the puff pastry on a lightly floured surface. Cut out a circle slightly larger than the pan.

Place the apples, peeled-side down, into the pan and sprinkle with the fresh thyme leaves. Pour over caramel mixture, cover with the pastry and tuck the overlapped edges down the side of the pan.

Bake in the oven for 20–25 minutes until the pastry is brown.

Remove the pan from the oven and leave to rest for 1 minute before turning it out. To do this, place a plate on top of the pan, and invert so that the tart slips out, pastry to the base, apples on the top. Serve hot with ice cream on the side.

150g caster sugar
25g butter
375g simple rough puff pastry (see page 13) or packet of fresh, ready-rolled all-butter puff pastry
flour, for rolling out
6 Golden Delicious apples, peeled, cored and cut into quarters
leaves from 2 thyme sprigs

This dessert was invented by French sisters Stephanie and Caroline Tatin. Stephanie was known for making an apple tart with a perfectly caramelized crust that melted in the mouth. One day she placed her tart in the oven upside down. Nevertheless, it was salvaged and served – and one of the most famous desserts of all was created.

fruit
MILLEFEUILLE

Preheat the oven to 180°C/350°F/Gas mark 4.

Roll the pastry on a lightly floured surface and cut out a rectangle measuring 12.5 x 31cm. Place on a non-stick baking tray and brush the top with the egg wash.

Bake in the oven for 15–20 minutes, until well-risen and golden brown. Remove from the oven, transfer to a wire rack and allow to cool.

Meanwhile, whip the cream, sugar and vanilla seeds to form soft peaks. Fold in the custard.

Once the pastry is cool, cut it in half horizontally and then spread the base with two-thirds of the cream mixture.

Toss all the prepared fruit together in a bowl, and sprinkle the fruit over the cream. Spread the remaining cream mixture over the bottom of the top side of pastry and then sandwich together. Dust generously with icing sugar to serve.

225g simple rough puff pastry (see page 13) or packet of fresh, ready-rolled all-butter puff pastry
flour, for rolling out
1 egg, beaten
150ml double cream
1 dsp icing sugar, sifted, plus extra for dusting
1 vanilla pod, split
75ml ready-made custard
300g raspberries
250g strawberries, hulled and cut in half
1 fig, chopped
100g blueberries

Millefeuille translates as 'dessert of a thousand layers'. It must be made with puff pastry, not filo which I've occasionally come across.

classic
LEMON TART

SERVES 8

Preheat the oven to 200°C/400°F/Gas mark 6.

To make the filling, break the eggs into a bowl and whisk gently to break up the yolks. Add the sugar and continue to mix, then add the cream and the lemon juice, but not the zest. Pass the mixture through a sieve, add the lemon zest and leave to one side.

Butter a 20cm plain, loose-bottomed flan tin with softened butter and roll out the pastry between two wooden rulers (if you have some) to get a thin but even depth to the pastry. Carefully roll the pastry back onto the rolling pin, lift over the tin and roll the pastry back over the tin very loosely. If you don't leave plenty of slack, the pastry will rip or shrink too much when cooking. Tuck the pastry down the sides of the tin, pressing into the bottom edge well, but be careful not to tear or stretch it. Don't trim the pastry.

Line the tart with a circle of greaseproof paper bigger than the tart to allow the paper to rise above the ring. Fill the tart with baking beans, rice or ceramic baking beans. Bake for about 10 minutes. Remove from the oven and remove the beans and paper, then put back in the oven to colour the bottom of the tart. This should only take 3–4 minutes.

Turn the oven down to 100°C/225°F/Gas mark ½. Pour in the lemon mix to reach the top of the tart and bake for about 1 hour until the tart is only just set. Remove from the oven and trim off the edges of the pastry. Leave to cool for about 1 hour. To make the accompanying cream, mix the goat cheese with the double cream and icing sugar.

To serve, dust the tart with plenty of icing sugar and grill under a hot grill to caramelize the top. Remove from the grill, cut into wedges and serve with a spoonful of the cream.

7 eggs
280g caster sugar
350ml double cream
zest and juice of 6 lemons
butter, for greasing
225g rich shortcrust pastry
   (see page 12)

To serve
100g mild goat cheese
50ml double cream
2 tbsp icing sugar,
   plus extra for dusting
a little whipped cream

french
FRUIT TART

SERVES 10

On a lightly floured surface, roll out the pastry and cut out a rectangle measuring 36 x 20cm. Place on a baking tray. Using a table knife, score a 1cm border around the edge, making sure you don't cut the pastry all the way through. Hold the knife like a pen, place your index finger against the outer edge of the pastry and run the knife along.

Brush the border with egg wash, taking care not to allow any to dribble down the sides because this will prevent the pastry from rising evenly. Prick the base of the tart (not the border) with a fork and chill the pastry for 20 minutes.

Preheat the oven to 200°C/400°F/Gas mark 6.

Bake the pastry for 20–25 minutes until golden brown and crisp. Slide onto a wire rack and leave to cool. Once cooled, gently press the centre of the pastry down to leave the frame around the edge.

Melt the chocolate and brush over the bottom of the pastry. Leave to set.

Add the vanilla seeds to the cream and fold in the custard. Spoon and spread the cream mixture over the pastry base. Draw shallow lines in the cream mixture to create five sections and arrange the fruit on top so that each section is a contrasting colour.

Heat the jam and, using a pastry brush, glaze the fruit. Allow to set before serving.

350g simple rough puff pastry
   (see page 13)
   or packet of fresh, ready-rolled
   all-butter puff pastry
plain flour, for rolling out
1 egg, beaten
85g white chocolate,
   broken into pieces
½ a vanilla pod, seeds only
200ml double cream,
   half-whipped
100ml fresh custard (see page 23)
small punnet of medium-sized
   strawberries, hulled and halved
small punnet of blackberries
   and raspberries
1 large banana, sliced
small bunch of seedless green
   and/or black grapes, halved
4 tbsp smooth apricot jam

truffle
TORTE

Line a 23cm cake tin with baking parchment and grease the base and sides with soft butter.

Crush the biscuits and put over the base of the tin.

Break the chocolate into squares and put them in a heatproof bowl, together with the liquid glucose and rum. Place the bowl over a pan of barely simmering water, making sure the base of the bowl doesn't touch the water, then leave it until the chocolate has melted and become quite smooth. Stir, then take off the heat and leave the mixture to cool slightly.

In a separate bowl beat the double cream until only very slightly thickened. Fold half into the chocolate mixture, then fold that mixture into the rest of the cream. When it is smoothly blended, spoon it into the prepared tin. Tap the tin gently to even out the mixture, cover with cling film and chill overnight.

Just before serving, run a warm knife round the edge to loosen the torte, then remove from the mould.

To serve, dust the surface with sifted cocoa powder and serve with single cream.

butter, for greasing
110g amaretti biscuits
450g dark chocolate
   (70–75% cocoa solids)
4 tbsp liquid glucose
4 tbsp rum
650ml double cream,
   at room temperature

To serve
cocoa powder, for dusting
single cream, chilled

prune &
ALMOND TART

Make the pastry as on page 13. Preheat the oven to 180°C/350°F/
Gas mark 4. Lightly grease four 10cm fluted, round, loose-bottomed
moulds, about 2.5cm deep.

To make the frangipane, cream the butter and sugar together until
almost white. Mix together the ground almonds and flour in a
separate bowl. Add one egg at a time to the butter and sugar mixture,
sprinkling in a handful of the almond-flour at the same time (this
helps the butter and sugar cream to mix in the eggs). Once all the eggs
have been added, drizzle with the brandy and continue to mix in the
remaining almond-flour.

Roll out the pastry and line the tart cases. Spread the jam on the base
of the tarts, then fill with the frangipane. Finish by sitting the prunes
on the top.

Bake for 30–35 minutes. Halfway through the cooking time, scatter
the flaked almonds onto the tarts. When cooked, remove from the
oven and allow to cool.

To serve, remove the tarts from their moulds and place on serving
plates. Spoon the ice cream on the side.

For the frangipane
225g unsalted butter
225g caster sugar
175g ground almonds
50g plain flour
4 eggs
4 tbsp brandy

For the tarts
200g rich shortcrust pastry
  (see page 12)
2 tbsp raspberry jam
275g frangipane (*see above*)
225g soft pitted prunes
10g flaked almonds
vanilla ice cream
  (see page 146), to serve

pumpkin
PIE

SERVES 8

For the pastry, sift the flour, icing sugar and salt into a large bowl. Add the butter and, using your fingertips, gently rub it into the flour. When the mixture is crumbly, add the chopped nuts, then sprinkle in the water and the egg yolk. Bring the pastry together (you may need to add more water) to make a smooth dough that will leave the bowl clean. Rest in the fridge for 30 minutes.

Cook the pumpkin in a steamer for 15–20 minutes, or until tender. Transfer to a blender and roughly purée.

Preheat the oven to 180°C/350°F/Gas mark 4. Lightly grease a 23cm x 4cm-deep loose-bottomed fluted tart tin. Roll out the pastry on a floured surface. Transfer it, rolling it over the pin, to the tin. Press lightly all over the base and sides of the tin, easing any overlapping pastry back down the sides. Trim, leaving 5mm above the rim of the tin. Prick the base all over with a fork and brush the pastry with the reserved egg white. Bake on a baking tray for 20–25 minutes until crisp and golden. (Check after 10 minutes – if the pastry has risen in the centre, prick it a few times and press it down again.)

Lightly whisk the eggs and extra yolk together in a large bowl. Put the molasses in a saucepan and heat gently. Add the sugar, spices and cream, then bring up to simmering point, whisking everything together. Pour it over the eggs and whisk again briefly. Add the pumpkin purée, still whisking to combine, then pour the filling into a jug.

When the pastry is ready, remove it from the oven. Pour half the filling in, return the tart to the oven and, with the oven shelf half out, pour in the rest of the filling. Slide the shelf back in. Bake the pie for 35–40 minutes, or until puffed up round the edge but still slightly wobbly in the centre. Cool on a wire rack. Serve chilled with crème fraîche.

For the pastry
175g plain flour, plus extra
　for rolling out
10g icing sugar
pinch of salt
75g butter, softened
40g pecans, roughly blitzed
　in a food processor
1–2 tbsp water
1 large egg yolk
1 egg white, lightly beaten

For the filling
450g (prepared weight) pumpkin
　flesh, cut into 2.5cm chunks
2 large eggs, plus 1 large yolk
1 tbsp molasses
75g soft dark brown sugar
1 tsp ground cinnamon
½ tsp freshly ground nutmeg
½ tsp ground allspice
½ tsp ground cloves
½ tsp ground ginger
275ml double cream

gooseberry
CRÈME FRAÎCHE TART

SERVES 6-8

Preheat the oven to 190°C/375°F/Gas mark 5. Lightly grease a 23cm x 2.5cm-deep, loose-bottomed tart tin.

Heat a baking tray in the oven while you roll out the pastry. Roll the pastry on a floured surface so that it is larger than the diameter of the tin. Line the tin with the pastry and prick the base all over with a fork. Brush the base and sides with some of the egg white leftover from the eggs for the filling. Place the pastry-lined tin on the hot baking tray (this will make the base cook).

Bake for 20 minutes until the pastry is just beginning to turn golden brown. Then remove it from the oven and reduce the heat to 180°C/ 350°F/Gas mark 4.

To make the filling, whisk the crème fraîche, egg yolks, whole egg and sugar together.

Carefully arrange the gooseberries in the pastry case, pour the crème fraîche mixture over the top and return the tart to the oven for 40–50 minutes, or until it's a light golden brown. Allow to cool before serving.

butter, for greasing
200g rich shortcrust pastry
    (see page 12)
flour, for rolling out

For the filling
200ml crème fraîche
4 large egg yolks
1 whole egg
100g caster sugar
450g gooseberries,
    topped and tailed

There is more to do with a gooseberry than a simple gooseberry fool. Not only is it a fantastic fruit for puddings, but it is particularly good for making into a chutney to serve with oily fish such as mackerel.

baked pear
& HONEY TART

SERVES 4-6

Preheat the oven to 180°C/350°F/Gas mark 4. Lightly grease a 24cm loose-bottomed tart tin.

Roll out the pastry into a circle 3mm thick and slightly wider than the tin. Line the tin, gently easing the pastry down into the corners. Leave 2.5cm pastry overhanging the edge. Chill for 10 minutes.

Line the pastry case with greaseproof paper and fill with dried beans, rice or flour. Put the tin onto a baking tray and bake for about 10 minutes. Remove the paper with the beans and bake the pastry case for a further 5 minutes, so that the pastry no longer looks glassy. Trim off the overhanging pastry edge level with the top of the tin.

Reduce the oven temperature to 170°C/325°F/Gas mark 3.

Peel, core and roughly slice six of the pears, Place in a pan with the water. Cook over a medium heat for 5–10 minutes, until soft. Sweeten with sugar to taste. Drain through a sieve to remove any excess liquid, then beat to a purée.

Peel and core the remaining two pears, and cut it into neat 6mm slices. Fry gently in the unsalted butter until softened and lightly coloured. Place the pear purée in the bottom of the pastry case and overlap the pear slices on top.

In a bowl, beat together the egg yolks, whole egg and honey, then whisk the double cream into the egg mix. Pour into the pastry case, over the pears, and bake for 30 minutes, until the mixture has set and is golden brown. Serve in slices with a dollop of cream.

400g rich shortcrust pastry
    (see page 12)
8 pears
1 tbsp water
caster sugar, to taste
20g unsalted butter,
    plus extra for greasing
4 medium egg yolks
1 medium whole egg
1 tbsp clear honey
600ml double cream
whipped cream, for serving

lemon
MERINGUE PIE

SERVES 8

Preheat the oven to 190°C/375°F/Gas mark 5. Grease a 23cm fluted loose-bottomed tin and place on a baking tray.

Make the pastry following the instructions for shortcrust pastry on page 12, then roll it out and line the tin.

Line the pastry case with greaseproof paper and fill with baking beans or flour. Blind-bake for 10 minutes. Remove from the oven and discard the greaseproof paper and flour or baking beans,

To make the lemon curd, bring 50ml water and the lemon juice to the boil in a saucepan. Dissolve the cornflour in a little water, then gradually pour the hot liquid onto the cornflour, whisking all the time until all incorporated and smooth. Return to the pan. Beat in the egg yolks, sugar and butter. Place back on the heat, add the zest and whisk for 30 seconds. Tip into the pastry case and leave to cool.

To make the meringue, follow the instructions for making hot meringue on page 20. Spoon the meringue into a piping bag with with a plain nozzle and pipe over the pastry case.

Use a cook's blowtorch to colour the meringue, then serve.

For the pastry base
110g cold unsalted butter, diced
225g plain white flour
a pinch of salt
2 tsp caster sugar
1 medium egg yolk
half an eggshell of cold water

For the lemon curd
zest and juice of 4 large lemons
5 tbsp cornflour
6 egg yolks
100g caster sugar
100g unsalted butter

For the meringue
6 medium egg whites
300g caster sugar

cakes &
BAKES

madeira
CAKE

SERVES 10

Preheat the oven to 180°C/350°F/Gas mark 4. Grease an 18cm round cake tin, then line the base with greaseproof paper and grease the paper.

Cream the butter and sugar together in a bowl until pale and fluffy. Beat in the eggs, one at a time, beating the mixture well between each one and adding a tablespoon of the flour with the last egg to prevent the mixture from curdling.

Sift the flour and gently fold in with enough milk to give a mixture that falls reluctantly from the spoon. Fold in the lemon zest.

Spoon the mixture into the prepared tin and lightly level the top. Bake on the middle shelf of the oven for 45–50 minutes, or until a warm skewer inserted into the centre comes out clean. Leave the cake to cool in the tin for 10 minutes, then turn it out onto a wire rack and leave to cool completely.

Meanwhile, make the candied peel. Dissolve the sugar in a saucepan with 50ml water, add the peel and simmer for 3–4 minutes. Remove from the heat and strain. Dust the cooled cake with icing sugar, then scatter the peel over the cake to decorate.

175g butter, at room temperature
175g caster sugar
3 large eggs
250g self-raising flour
approximately 3 tbsp full-fat milk
finely grated zest of 1 lemon
icing sugar, for dusting

For the candied peel
finely shredded peel of
    half a lemon
50g sugar

Confusingly, Madeira cake doesn't come from the island of Madeira. It's an English cake, often called pound cake, dating back to the nineteenth century. It was, however, always served with Madeira wine. Either way, it tastes great.

butterfly
CAKES

Preheat the oven to 180°C/350°F/Gas mark 4. Line a 12-hole cake tin with paper cases.

Cream the butter, sugar and vanilla extract together in a bowl until pale. Gradually add the eggs and beat to combine.

Sift the flour into the mixture and fold to combine. Spoon into the cases and bake in the preheated oven for 20–25 minutes, until golden brown and springy to the touch.

Remove from the oven and transfer to a wire rack to cool.

Meanwhile, whip the cream and vanilla seeds in a bowl to form soft peaks. Transfer to a piping bag fitted with a star nozzle.

Carefully slice off the domed tops of the fairy cakes. Cut the tops in half to form semi-circles and set aside. Pipe a little of the cream mixture onto the cut side of the cake. Press the two cake semi-circles into the cream, cut-side down, to create butterfly wings.

Dust with icing sugar before serving.

175g unsalted butter, softened
175g caster sugar
few drops of vanilla extract
4 medium eggs
175g self-raising flour

For the filling
250ml double cream,
1 vanilla pod, split
icing sugar, for dusting

If you're a complete beginner, this is where you should start in this book – the recipe is so simple.

swiss
ROLL

SERVES 6-8

Preheat the oven to 200°C/400°F/Gas mark 6. Grease a 2 x 22 x 32cm Swiss roll tin and line with greaseproof paper.

Put the eggs, half the sugar and vanilla extract into a bowl or food mixer and whisk until pale and thickened.

Put the remaining sugar on a baking tray and warm in the oven for just a few minutes. Once the egg and sugar mixture has thickened, add the warm sugar to the bowl and continue to whisk until it is well-combined.

Sift the flour into the bowl and fold together. Pour the sponge mixture into the prepared tin and bake for 10–12 minutes, until golden and springy to the touch.

Place a sheet of greaseproof paper on a damp tea towel and dust generously with caster sugar. Turn the sponge out onto the paper and remove the base lining. Leave to cool.

For the filling, whip the cream with the seeds from the vanilla pod. Spread the jam over the cake, then spread a layer of cream on top. Carefully roll up with the aid of the paper. Make sure the first turn is tight so that the cake will roll evenly.

Transfer the Swiss roll to a serving plate and dust with caster sugar before serving.

butter, for greasing
4 medium eggs
125g caster sugar,
    plus extra for dusting
few drops of vanilla extract
125g plain flour

For the filling
250ml double cream
half a vanilla pod, seeds only
150g strawberry or raspberry jam

chocolate fudge
CAKE

SERVES 6-8

Preheat the oven to 170°C/325°F/Gas mark 3. Lightly grease a 20cm springform cake tin and line the base with baking parchment.

Weigh the flour, then take out 1 rounded tablespoon and replace it with the rounded tablespoon of cocoa. (The tablespoon of flour you remove won't be needed.)

Add the baking powder to the flour and cocoa, tip into a bowl, add the remaining cake ingredients and beat them together. You will end up with a mixture that drops off a spoon when you give it a whack on the side of the bowl. If the mixture seems a little too stiff, add a little water and mix again.

Spread the mixture evenly in the prepared tin and bake on the centre shelf of the oven for about 40–45 minutes, or until springy in the centre. Remove from the oven and, after about 30 seconds, turn the cake out onto a wire cooling rack and strip off the base paper. Once cool, carefully cut the cake in half horizontally and set aside.

For the filling, combine the sugar and evaporated milk in a heavy saucepan. Heat gently to dissolve the sugar, stirring frequently. When the sugar has dissolved and the mixture comes to the boil, keep the heat very low and simmer for 6 minutes without stirring. Remove the pan from the heat and, using a small balloon whisk, whisk in the chocolate, followed by the butter and vanilla extract.

Transfer the mixture to a bowl and, when it is cool, cover it with cling film and chill for about 1 hour to allow the mixture to thicken. Then beat again and spread half on one sponge, placing the other sponge on top. Spread the remainder over the top and sides. Decorate the top with the almonds and dust with cocoa powder or icing sugar to serve.

For the cake
175g very soft butter,
    plus extra for greasing
175g self-raising wholemeal flour
1 rounded tbsp cocoa powder
1 rounded tsp baking powder
175g light soft brown sugar
3 large eggs, at room temperature

For the filling and topping
125g light soft brown sugar
170g tin of evaporated milk
125g dark chocolate (50–55%
    cocoa solids), broken into
    small pieces
50g butter, softened
2 drops vanilla extract

To decorate
flaked almonds
cocoa powder or icing sugar,
    for dusting

sachertorte

Preheat the oven to 150°C/300°F/Gas mark 2. Lightly grease a 20cm springform cake tin and line the base with baking parchment.

Melt the chocolate slowly in a heatproof bowl set over a saucepan of barely simmering water (make sure the base of the bowl doesn't touch the water).

Using an electric hand whisk, cream the butter and sugar until very pale and fluffy. Beat in the egg yolks a little at a time, whisking well after each addition.

When the chocolate has cooled slightly, fold it gradually into the creamed butter mixture and then add the vanilla. Add the flour and baking powder and carefully fold it in with a large metal spoon.

Whisk the egg whites in a large, clean bowl to the stiff-peak stage which will take a few minutes, then carefully fold them into the mixture, little by little, using a metal spoon.

Pour the mixture into the prepared cake tin, level the top and bake on the middle shelf of the oven for about 1 hour, or until firm and well risen. When cooked, allow the cake to cool in the tin for 10 minutes before turning it out onto a cooling rack, then leave it to get quite cold. Warm the apricot jam and brush the cake all over with it.

To make the icing, melt the chocolate with the cream, also in a bowl over simmering water. Then remove the bowl from the heat and stir in the glucose to give a coating consistency. Pour the icing over the whole cake, making sure it covers the top and sides completely. Leave to set for a few hours before serving.

For the cake
110g soft butter,
    plus extra for greasing
175g dark chocolate
110g caster sugar
4 large egg yolks, lightly beaten
a dash of vanilla extract
125g plain flour
½ tsp baking powder
5 large egg whites
4 tsp smooth apricot jam

For the icing
175g dark chocolate
150ml double cream
2 tsp glucose

wedding
CAKE

SERVES 25-30

Preheat the oven to 180°C/350°F/Gas mark 4.

For the large sponge, lightly butter a 30cm cake tin and line the base with greaseproof paper. Cream the butter and sugar until smooth and pale in colour and then gradually beat in the eggs. Sift the flour and fold into the mixture, a little at a time. Pour into the cake tin, level off the mixture with a palette knife and bake for about 1½ hours, or until a skewer inserted into the cake comes out clean. Cool on a wire rack.

For the small sponge, lightly butter a 24cm cake tin and line the base with greaseproof paper. Mix the sponge in the same way but only bake for about 45 minutes.

To assemble the cake, place the large sponge cake onto a cake board, serving plate or cake stand, then position the smaller sponge cake centrally on top.

To make the buttercream, beat the butter and icing sugar together in a large bowl until almost white. Spread the buttercream generously over both cakes. Stick the white chocolate curls upright around the edge of each cake.

Push the stems of the roses and ivy into the foil-covered oasis to make a pretty arrangement. Carefully place the flower arrangement on top of the cake, securing it with cocktail sticks if necessary.

For the large sponge
700g butter,
    plus extra for greasing
700g caster sugar
12 medium eggs
650g self-raising flour

For the small sponge
275g butter
275g caster sugar
6 medium eggs
275g self-raising flour

For the buttercream
500g unsalted butter, softened
500g icing sugar

For the decoration
2 boxes of white chocolate curls
small roses in a variety of colours
ivy leaves
5cm block of florist's oasis,
    covered in foil

carrot
CAKE

Preheat the oven to 190°C/375°F/Gas mark 5. Lightly grease a 25cm, 6cm deep cake tin and line the base with baking parchment.

To make the cake, mix the sugar, eggs and oil in a bowl with an electric hand whisk for 3–4 minutes until smooth. Sift the flour, mixed spice and bicarbonate of soda into the bowl, tipping in any bits left in the sieve. Stir together gently, then add the remaining cake ingredients.

Pour the cake mixture evenly into the tin and bake on the centre oven shelf for 35–40 minutes. It should be nicely risen and feel firm and springy when lightly pressed in the centre. If not, give it a few minutes and test again. Remove the cake from the tin and cool on a wire rack.

Mix all the icing ingredients together in a bowl until light and fluffy. Cover with cling film and leave in the fridge until time to ice the cake.

For the decoration, trim the green carrot stalks to 2.5cm long. Put them in a saucepan and just cover with cold water. Add the salt, sugar and butter, bring to the boil and boil quickly for 5–6 minutes. The carrots cook as the water evaporates, forming a glaze in the bottom of the pan. Coat in the glaze, remove from the pan and leave to cool.

To make the banana tuiles, purée the banana in a mini blender, add the egg white and whiz together. Spread the batter onto silicone paper on a baking tray in a very thin layer in the desired shapes. Bake in the oven at 180°C/350°F/Gas mark 4 for 20–30 minutes until brown. Remove the tuiles from the tray while still hot and leave to cool.

To decorate, spread the icing roughly over the top of the cake. Garnish the top with the banana tuiles, sugared carrots and lengths of pulled sugar.

For the cake
175g dark soft brown sugar
2 large eggs
150ml olive oil (not virgin olive oil)
200g wholemeal self-raising flour
1 tbsp ground mixed spice
1 tsp bicarbonate of soda
200g carrots, peeled and grated
80g pecans, roughly chopped
grated zest of 1 lemon
110g sultanas
25g raisins
50g desiccated coconut

For the icing
250g mascarpone
250ml double cream
2 tbsp icing sugar

For the carrot decoration
300g baby carrots (washed)
1 tsp salt
70g sugar
50g butter

For the banana tuiles
1 ripe banana, peeled and chopped
1 medium egg white

To decorate
spun sugar (see pages 18–19)

gateau
SAINT-HONORÉ

SERVES 8-10

Preheat the oven to 180°C/350°F/Gas mark 4. Line two baking trays with parchment. Place a 23cm metal ring on one of the lined trays.

Make the choux pastry recipe as on pages 14–15. Transfer the pastry to a piping bag, and use half to pipe into 12 small buns on one of the baking trays. Pipe the remaining half into the metal ring on the other baking tray. Transfer the baking trays to the oven and cook for 10–15 minutes, until risen and golden. Set aside to cool.

Next, whip up the double cream until firm, split the vanilla pod and add the seeds only to the cream. Fold the custard into the cream together with 2 tbsp of the sugar and a dash of orange liqueur.

Heat the remaining sugar in a non-stick pan over a medium heat and cook to a caramel. If the mixture begins to set, warm up gently.

Once the sugar has been caramelized, carefully dip each choux bun into the sugar and then place on a greased baking tray to cool.

Remove the ring from the pastry base and drizzle the remaining liqueur over the middle. Using an ice-cream scoop or a tablespoon warmed in hot water, place half the custard and cream mixture into the centre of the base.

Use the remaining cream mixture to fill the choux buns and arrange the buns around the edge of the flan. Garnish one side with the roses and twigs and serve.

1 quantity of choux pastry
   (see pages 14–15)
300ml double cream
1 vanilla pod, seeds only
200ml fresh custard
100g caster sugar
50ml orange liqueur

To garnish
10–12 small white and pink roses
small twisted twigs

grandma's caramel
SHORTBREAD

MAKES ABOUT 6

First, make the caramel. Place the tin of condensed milk in a deep saucepan and cover it with water. Bring to the boil, then reduce the heat and cover with a lid. Leave to simmer rapidly for 2 hours (keep an eye on the water level). Allow it to cool completely before you open the tin, where you'll find a golden sticky caramel. (Once cooked, a tin of caramelized condensed milk will keep in the fridge for 2 weeks.)

Preheat the oven to 170°C/340°F/Gas mark 3½. Line a 20 x 30cm baking tin with baking parchment.

Cream the butter with the sugar until light and fluffy. Sift together the flours, then mix with the butter and sugar. Gently knead the dough until it comes together in a firm ball.

Roll out two-thirds of the dough to fit the tin and lay it inside, pressing it neatly into the edges. Spread three-quarters of the condensed milk caramel evenly over the base. Crumble the remaining dough over the top of the caramel.

Bake for 20 minutes. The caramel should bubble up a little between the dough and the top of the shortbread should be golden. Leave to cool in the tin for 5 minutes, then cut into squares. Finish cooling in the tin.

To serve, reheat the squares for 5 minutes at 160°C/325°F/Gas mark 3. Finish with a sprig of fresh mint, a dollop of vanilla ice cream and a drizzle of the remaining caramel sauce.

1 x 397g tin of condensed milk
250g unsalted butter,
    at room temperature
150g caster sugar
150g cornflour
300g flour

lardy
CAKE

Blend the fresh yeast with the warm water (don't use hot water as this would kill the yeast; cold water can be used but the dough would take longer to prove).

Put the flour and salt in a bowl and rub in one-third of the lard. Make a well in the centre and pour in the yeast liquid. Mix together to make a dough that leaves the sides of the bowl clean (add a bit more water if necessary).

Turn onto a lightly floured surface and knead well for about 5 minutes, until smooth and elastic. Place in a clean bowl. Cover with a clean tea towel and leave in a warm place for about 1 hour, until doubled in size. Turn the dough onto a floured surface and roll out to a rectangle about 5mm thick. Dot one-third of the remaining lard and one-third of the butter over the surface of the dough. Sprinkle over one-third of the fruit, peel and sugar. Fold the dough in three, folding the bottom third up and the top third down. Give a quarter turn, then repeat the process twice more, using up the remaining ingredients.

Grease a 20 x 25cm baking tin. Roll the dough out to fit the prepared tin. Put it into the tin, cover and leave in a warm place for 30 minutes until it rises.

Preheat the oven to 220°C/425°F/Gas mark 7. Score the top of the dough in a criss-cross pattern using a very sharp knife, then bake in the oven for about 30 minutes until golden brown. Turn out and serve warm.

15g fresh yeast
275ml warm water
450g strong white flour
2 pinches of salt
75g lard, diced
75g butter, diced
100g sultanas
75g currants
50g chopped mixed peel
50g caster sugar

chocolate cola
CAKE

SERVES 8

Preheat the oven to 180°C/350°F/Gas mark 4. Grease a 24cm loose-bottomed cake tin.

Sift the flour, sugar, cocoa and bicarbonate of soda into a bowl. Gently melt the butter and cola drink together in a pan, then add to the dry ingredients, together with the milk, eggs and vanilla extract. Mix gently but thoroughly, then tip into the cake tin.

Bake for about 40 minutes, or until a skewer inserted into the centre of the cake comes out clean. Remove from the oven and leave to cool on a wire rack for about 15 minutes while you make the topping.

To make the topping, beat the butter, icing sugar and cocoa together in a bowl until blended. Beat in the cola to combine. Spread over the cake and allow the topping to set.

To make the sauce, melt the chocolate bar gently in a pan with a splash of cream (you may want to add a little warm water to achieve a pouring consistency), then stir in the marshmallows, if using. The sauce is rich and sweet, as is the topping, so you may want to serve with one or the other rather than both.

This recipe sounds odd but it tastes great and is so moist when cooked – I love it. If you prefer a thicker frosting, double the quantities for the topping.

250g butter,
    plus extra for greasing
250g self-raising flour
300g golden caster sugar
3 heaped tbsp cocoa
generous pinch of
    bicarbonate of soda
200ml cola drink
75ml milk
2 eggs, beaten
1 tsp vanilla extract

For the topping
60g butter, softened
200g icing sugar, sifted
2–3 tbsp cocoa
2 tbsp cola drink

For the sauce
king-sized caramel
    chocolate bar
splash of double cream
2 tbsp mini marshmallows
    (optional)

macadamia nut
CHOCOLATE CAKE

SERVES 6

Preheat the oven to 180°C/350°F/Gas mark 4. Butter 6 ring moulds 5cm wide by 2.5cm deep. Place on a parchment-lined baking tray.

Finely grind half the macadamia nuts and coarsely chop the rest.

Cream the butter and sugar together and add the eggs one at a time, mixing well after each addition. Add the cocoa, flour and baking powder and stir until fully incorporated. Gently fold the ground nuts into the batter.

Fill the moulds two-thirds full with the batter and sprinkle with the chopped macadamia nuts.

Bake for 15–20 minutes, or until a skewer inserted into the centre comes out clean.

To make the sauce, gently heat the chocolate and butter in a saucepan until melted, stir in the cream and sugar and continue to heat gently, stirring, until combined.

To serve, pour a pool of chocolate sauce onto each plate. Place a cake in the centre of each plate on top of the sauce. Spoon the ice cream to the side.

75g toasted macadamia nuts
190g unsalted butter
200g sugar
4 eggs
45g unsweetened cocoa, sifted
70g plain flour
¼ tsp baking powder

For the chocolate sauce
25g bittersweet
   chocolate, chopped
1 tbsp unsalted butter
4 tbsp double cream
15g sugar

To serve
vanilla ice cream (see page 146)

These cakes must be served warm as they become more like a muffin when cold. If necessary, give them a quick blast in the microwave for 10 seconds to bring them back to full glory.

chocolate chip
COOKIES

MAKES 30

Preheat the oven to 180°C/350°F/Gas mark 4. Line two 28 x 35cm baking trays with baking parchment.

Put the butter and sugar in a mixing bowl and beat together with an electric hand whisk until light and fluffy.

Split the vanilla pod lengthways. Using the end of a teaspoon or a small sharp knife, scoop out the seeds. Beat the egg and the vanilla seeds into the mixture, then add the remaining ingredients and stir until thoroughly mixed.

Take spoonfuls of the dough (about the size of a walnut) and arrange them on the baking trays, spaced well apart.

Bake them on the shelf just above the centre of the oven for 10 minutes, or until the cookies have turned a golden colour and feel firm in the centre when lightly pressed.

As soon as the cookies are baked, remove them from the baking sheets using a palette knife. Cool them on a wire rack and, when cold, store in an airtight container.

110g butter, softened
110g light muscovado sugar
1 vanilla pod, seeds only
1 medium egg, lightly beaten
75g plain wholemeal flour
110g dark chocolate chips
50g toasted hazelnuts, chopped

dark chocolate
BROWNIES

Preheat the oven to 170°C/325°F/Gas mark 3. Grease and flour a 23cm square cake tin. Line the base with greaseproof paper.

Melt the butter and chocolate together in a heatproof bowl set over a pan of simmering water.

Whisk the eggs together and slowly add the sugar. Beat in the chocolate mixture and gently fold in the flour, baking powder and pinch of salt.

Pour the mixture into the tin. Bake in the oven for 40–45 minutes until the surface is set. It is cooked when a skewer placed in the middle comes out with a little of the mixture sticking to it.

Remove from the oven and cool in the tin slightly, then place on a wire rack and leave to cool.

Cut the cake into squares and keep in a tin or in the fridge.

250g unsalted butter, plus extra for greasing
100g plain flour, sieved, plus extra for flouring tin
350g dark chocolate
3 medium eggs
250g dark muscovado sugar
1 tsp baking powder
pinch of salt

There are stacks of brownie recipes around. This one originally came from an old American pastry chef I once knew. If you have any broken brownies leftover, mix them into some vanilla ice cream or sprinkle them over the top when serving.

buttermilk
SCONES

Preheat the oven to 220°C/425°F/Gas mark 7. Lightly grease a baking tray.

Sift the flour and salt into a bowl, rub the butter lightly into the mixture until it looks like breadcrumbs, then add the sugar. Beat the egg and 2 tablespoons of the buttermilk together in another bowl, then start to add this to the flour mixture, mixing the dough with a palette knife. When it begins to come together, finish off with your hands – it should be soft but not sticky.

When you have formed the dough into a ball, tip it onto a lightly floured surface and roll it into a circle at least 2.5cm thick – be very careful not to roll it any thinner as the secret of well-risen scones is to start off with a thickness of no less than 2.5cm.

Cut out the scones by placing a 5cm plain-edge cutter on the dough and giving it a sharp tap – don't twist it, just lift it up and push the dough out. Carry on until you are left with the trimmings, then bring these back together to roll out again so you can cut out one last scone.

Turn the scones over and place on the baking tray, brush them lightly with buttermilk and dust with a little flour. Bake on the top shelf of the oven for 10–12 minutes, or until they are well risen and golden brown, then remove them to a wire rack to cool. Serve with clotted cream and any jam or jelly that takes your fancy.

75g butter, at room temperature, plus extra for greasing
225g self-raising flour, plus a little extra for rolling out and dusting
pinch of salt
40g caster sugar
1 large egg, beaten
2 tbsp buttermilk, plus a little extra for brushing
clotted cream and jam, for serving

Buttermilk can be used as an alternative to milk when making cakes and in baking in general.

jam
SHORTBREADS

Preheat the oven to 180°C/350°F/Gas mark 4.

Sift the icing sugar, flour and cornflour together into a bowl. Add the ground almonds and butter. Using your fingers, a mixer or food processor, rub or mix the butter in until there are no visible lumps of butter.

Add the almond essence. Turn the mixture out onto a lightly floured surface and knead a few times, just to form a smooth dough.

Cover a baking tray with a non-stick baking mat and place a 6cm metal ring on top. Roll the dough into 20–24 small balls and place one inside the metal ring, push it down and flatten the top slightly with your fingers. Repeat with the remaining dough.

Bake the shortbreads for 8–12 minutes until they are a light golden colour. Remove them from the oven and, using a round kitchen tool, such as the end of a wooden spoon handle, make a small indentation in the top of each biscuit.

Let the shortbreads cool for a few minutes, then neaten the edges of the biscuits by re-cutting with the metal ring. Be gentle, as they are fragile while they are still warm. Transfer to a wire rack to cool.

When cooled, dust the tops with some icing sugar in a shaker or sieve. Using a teaspoon, fill the indentation with a little jam or your chosen filling.

90g icing sugar
185g plain flour
60g cornflour
30g ground almonds
250g butter, cut into cubes
½ tsp almond essence
caster sugar, for dusting
raspberry or strawberry jam

apple & toffee
MUFFINS

Preheat the oven to 190°C/375°F/Gas mark 5. Line a 12-hole bun or muffin tin with paper cases.

Mix the eggs, sugar, milk and melted butter in a large bowl. Sift in the flour, baking powder, salt and cinnamon. Add the chopped apple and mix roughly.

Spoon the mixture into the muffin cases, filling them a quarter full, then top with a few pieces of toffee, and cover with the rest of the muffin mixture until the paper cases are half-full.

Bake in the oven for 30–35 minutes until well risen and golden. Cool on a wire rack.

2 eggs, beaten
80g caster sugar
240ml milk
100g butter, melted
300g plain flour
2 tsp baking powder
½ tsp salt
good pinch of cinnamon
2 eating apples, such as Cox or Granny Smiths, peeled, cored and finely chopped
50g toffee, broken into small pieces

Don't put too much toffee in each of the muffins or it will boil over during baking. For a different flavour, try using nutmeg instead of cinnamon. These muffins also make a great pudding when served with vanilla ice cream.

ice creams
& SORBETS

chocolate
SORBET

SERVES 4

Place the milk, sugar, glucose and cocoa in a saucepan with the water.

Heat gently, whisking all the time, until the mixture boils, then add the chopped chocolate.

Allow the chocolate to melt, then pass the mixture through a sieve and allow to cool.

When cool, churn in an ice-cream machine until set.

Once frozen, transfer the sorbet from the machine into a freezerproof container with a lid and store in the freezer. The sorbet will keep for a few months.

200ml milk
100g caster sugar
50g liquid glucose
20g cocoa powder
200ml water
160g dark chocolate, chopped

When buying chocolate for cooking, always buy the best you can afford – but avoid sweet chocolate bars.

brown bread
ICE CREAM

Preheat the oven to 200°C/400°F/Gas mark 6.

Spread the breadcrumbs out on a baking tray and toast in the oven for a couple of minutes until crisp and slightly browned.

Meanwhile, beat the two creams with the sugar. Mix together the yolks and rum, if using, and add to the cream mixture, beating it in well.

When the breadcrumbs are cool, fold them gently into the cream mixture, making sure they are evenly distributed.

Lastly, whip the whites of the eggs until stiff and fold into the mixture. Transfer to a sealable container, place in the freezer and store until needed. (There is no need to stir this ice cream while it freezes.)

175g brown wholemeal
   breadcrumbs
300ml double cream
300ml single cream
125g icing sugar
2 egg yolks
1 tbsp rum (optional)
2 egg whites

Who would have thought that brown bread in desserts would add so much flavour? Yet it's the bread that makes this ice cream taste so good.

vanilla
ICE CREAM
SERVES 6-8

Using a sharp knife, cut the vanilla pod in half lengthways and remove the seeds. Put the milk, vanilla seeds and pod, half the caster sugar and the cream in a pan and bring to the boil.

Whisk the egg yolks in a bowl and add the remaining sugar.

When the cream mixture has boiled, pour it slowly onto the eggs, whisking all the time. Return the mixture to the pan over a high heat and mix quickly until the mixture has thickened. Pass through a sieve into a bowl, then put the mixture into an ice-cream machine. Churn until the ice cream has set.

Once set, transfer the ice cream into a sealable container, place in the freezer and store until needed.

To make the almond ice cream featured on pages 50–51, reduce the quantity of caster sugar to 150g and add 75–100ml amaretto and 50g toasted flaked almonds.

1 vanilla pod
500ml milk
200g caster sugar
500ml double cream
8 egg yolks

This standard ice cream recipe can be adapted to different flavours simply by removing the vanilla pod and replacing with zest and juice, or a juicy fruit such as passion fruit. However, if you're making a honey- or alcohol-flavoured ice cream, remove 50g of sugar – too much sugar or alcohol acts as a defrosting agent.

white chocolate
ICE CREAM

Whisk the egg yolks and caster sugar together in a bowl until pale and fluffy.

Bring the milk up to the boil in a pan.

Put the chocolate into a large bowl and leave to one side.

Pour the hot milk onto the egg yolks and whisk together. Return to the pan and heat, stirring all the time until the mixture thickens.

Pass the hot mixture through a sieve onto the chocolate and allow the mixture to cool.

Mix in the cream, put in an ice-cream machine and churn until set. Transfer to a sealable container, place in the freezer and store until needed.

12 egg yolks
200g caster sugar
600ml milk
250g white chocolate, chopped
600ml double cream

Make sure you use good-quality white chocolate and not standard sweet bars of white chocolate, as these are full of other ingredients which will cause the mixture to go grainy in texture when churned.

fresh mango
SORBET

Peel and stone the mangoes. Dice the flesh into pieces and place in a blender or food processor. Add the icing sugar and lemon juice and blend to a purée.

Place into an ice-cream machine and churn to freeze.

Once frozen, transfer from the machine into a sealable container and store in the freezer until required. The sorbet will keep for a few months.

This recipe will also work well with strawberries and many other fruits that can be made into a purée. Whichever fruit you choose, do use the lemon juice as it adds to the taste. In total, you will need about 900ml of liquid purée for this quantity of sugar. For a softer style of sorbet, add a whipped egg white to the mix when the churning stage is nearly complete.

3 fresh mangoes
250g icing sugar, sifted
juice of 2 lemons

junket
ICE CREAM

SERVES 10

Put the eggs and sugar into a bowl and whisk to combine.

Put the cream, milk and split vanilla pod into a saucepan and bring to a boil. Pour onto the eggs and sugar and whisk.

Return to the saucepan and bring to a boil, stirring constantly. Cook for about 1 minute, until just thickened, then remove from the heat. Pass the mixture through a sieve into a bowl and add the rum.

Pour into an ice-cream machine and churn until frozen.

Transfer the mixture to a sealable container, place in the freezer and freeze until required.

8 eggs
180g caster sugar
250ml double cream
750ml milk
1 vanilla pod
6 tbsp rum

Junket is an old-fashioned dish. Roughly speaking, it is made from warmed milk with rennet added and allowed to set, sometimes flavoured with rum or vanilla. Here I've taken the flavours and milk and made it into ice cream. Served with other old classic puds like spotted dick (see page 34), it tastes great.

lemon
GRANITA

Put the caster sugar into a saucepan with the water and bring to the boil. Simmer for 5 minutes, then leave to cool.

Add the lemon zest and juice to the sugar syrup.

Pour into a freezerproof container and freeze for 3 hours, stirring every 15 minutes to prevent the mixture freezing into a solid block.

250g caster sugar
500ml water
zest of 2 lemons
juice of 4 lemons

Granita is related to sorbet as it's a semi-frozen dessert made from water, sugar and flavourings. It originates from Italy and that's where I've eaten some of the best, probably due to the quality of the lemons. The texture of granitas varies so much; if churned in a machine it will become smoother, but if forked through it will be a chunkier example.

20-second strawberry
ICE CREAM

Tip the frozen strawberry pieces into a food processor. Add the vanilla extract, sugar and half the buttermilk.

Turn on the processor and let it run for a few moments. Then, while it is still running, pour in the remaining buttermilk in a thin, steady stream. Let the machine run until the mixture is beautifully smooth and creamy. Don't overmix as this will cause the ice cream to defrost.

Serve straight away with mixed fresh berries.

400g whole strawberries, with the green removed and frozen (see below)
dash of vanilla extract
30g caster sugar
150ml buttermilk
200g mixed berries, to serve (optional)

If there is such a thing as no-fat ice cream, this has to be it. The only downside is that it doesn't refreeze once made. Freeze the whole strawberries on a baking tray so that you have separate frozen fruits, rather than a solid block of them.

apple
SORBET

SERVES 6

Quarter and core the apples, but do not peel. Toss them in a bowl with the lemon juice. Put in a single layer in a shallow plastic container and freeze for at least 1 hour.

Dissolve the sugar in the water in a heavy-based saucepan over a low heat. Bring to the boil and cook over a medium heat for 5 minutes. Cool, then mix in the glucose.

Whiz the ice-cold apples in a food processor, gradually adding about a third of the syrup to make a fine purée. Scrape down the sides of the bowl once or twice as you do this. Mix in the rest of the syrup.

Transfer the mixture to an ice-cream machine. Churn until almost solid, then transfer to a rigid plastic container, seal and freeze until required. Serve in scoops.

4 large Granny Smith apples
juice of 1 large lemon
200g caster sugar
400ml water
4 tbsp liquid glucose

USEFUL ADDRESSES

SPECIALIST KITCHEN EQUIPMENT

Leon Jaeggi
77 Shaftesbury Avenue
London W1D 5DU
020 7580 1974

Nisbets
Fourth Way
Avonmouth
Bristol BS11 8TB
0845 140 5555
www.nisbets.co.uk

Pages Catering
121 Shaftesbury Avenue
London WC2H 8AD
0845 373 4017

GREAT DELIS

Cadogan & James Deli
31 The Square
Winchester
Hampshire SO23 9EX
01962 877399
www.jamesmartinchef.co.uk
www.cadoganandcompany.co.uk

Fanny's Farm Shop
Markedge Lane
Merstham
Redhill
Surrey RH1 3AW
01737 554444
www.fannysfarm.com

Fenwick
39 Northumberland Street
Newcastle upon Tyne NE99 1AR
0191 232 5100
www.fenwick.co.uk/newcastle

**Lucy's of Ambleside and
'Up the Duff Pudding Night'**
Church Street
Ambleside
Cumbria LA22 0BU
01539 432288
www.lucysofambleside.co.uk

Partridges of Sloane Square
2–5 Duke of York Square
London SW3 4LY
020 7730 0651
www.partridges.co.uk

GOOD-QUALITY CHOCOLATE AND SUGARCRAFT SUPPLIES

Chocolate Trading Company
The Old School
Byron Street
Macclesfield
Cheshire SK11 7QA
08700 508244
www.chocolatetradingco.com

The Craft Company
Unit 4 Hermes Court
Hermes Close
Warwick CV34 6NJ
01926 888507
www.craftcompany.co.uk

Imaginative Icing
22 Falsgrave Road
Scarborough
North Yorkshire YO12 5AT
01723 378116
www.imaginativeicing.co.uk

William Curley Chocolatier
10 Paved Court
Richmond upon Thames
Surrey TW9 1LZ
020 8332 3002
www.williamcurley.com

INDEX

EVERYWHERE I GO IN BRITAIN, people ask me when I'm going to write a book on desserts. With the great support of Elaine Bedell and Roly Keating of BBC 2, I have a fantastic series on desserts and an accompanying book. Thanks to Jane Lush, Fenia Vardinas, Emma Robertson, David Vallance, Steve Moss and Andy Muggleton at Splash Media. My excellent assistant on the series, Will Torrent, has provided brilliant support throughout and is a talent to look out for! Huge thanks also to Lisa Harrison, Chris Start and Pippa Bull – I hope they haven't piled on too many pounds during the creation of this book! No worries, guys – the treadmills are on order! Jane O'Shea, Helen Lewis, Gillian Haslam and Gabriella Le Grazie of Quadrille must also be applauded for their tireless support and efforts that went into making this book happen. Denby, Stellar and Wahl provided the equipment for the series – cheers, guys! Thanks also to Barbara Prince and her team at Aston Martin. As ever, I want to say a big thank you to my agency team at Limelight Management, who have been there for me when I needed them (and when I didn't!): Fiona Lindsay, Linda Shanks, Mary Bekhait and Alison Lindsay. Last but not least, I want to say a big thank you to the photographer, Peter Cassidy, and his assistant, Colin, for the stonking photographs.

For further information, visit www.jamesmartinchef.co.uk